*Jacobus Arminius
Stands His Ground*

Jacobus Arminius Stands His Ground

A Declaration against High Calvinism

John S. Knox

Foreword by Roger J. Newell

Afterword by Vic Reasoner

WIPF & STOCK · Eugene, Oregon

JACOBUS ARMINIUS STANDS HIS GROUND
A Declaration against High Calvinism

Copyright © 2018 John S. Knox. All rights reserved. Except for brief quotations in critical publications or reviews, no part of this book may be reproduced in any manner without prior written permission from the publisher. Write: Permissions, Wipf and Stock Publishers, 199 W. 8th Ave., Suite 3, Eugene, OR 97401.

Wipf & Stock
An Imprint of Wipf and Stock Publishers
199 W. 8th Ave., Suite 3
Eugene, OR 97401

www.wipfandstock.com

PAPERBACK ISBN: 978-1-5326-3371-3
HARDCOVER ISBN: 978-1-5326-3373-7
EBOOK ISBN: 978-1-5326-3372-0

Manufactured in the U.S.A.   NOVEMBER 2, 2018

Lovingly dedicated to my favorite boss of all time,

Thomas Mostul, and his sweet wife, Eileen,

for their kind and generous support of me while in Seminary.

Contents

List of Illustrations | *viii*

Foreword by Roger J. Newell | *xi*

Preface | *xv*

Acknowledgments | *xix*

1. Introduction | 1
2. The Cultural Surroundings of Arminius and a Declaration | 5
3. Principal Characters in the Development of a Declaration | 12
4. Overview of A Declaration of Sentiments | 32
5. Detailed Analysis of A Declaration of Sentiments | 37
6. Scholarly Voices on A Declaration of Sentiments | 55
7. Reflections Upon the Man and His Manuscript | 66
8. Final Thoughts | 72

Afterword by Vic Reasoner | *76*

Glossary | *81*

Additional Notes on a Declaration | *87*

Bibliography | *93*

Index | *99*

Illustrations

Figure 1: Reformation-Era Europe | 4

Figure 2: Timeline | 11

Figure 3: The Netherlands (Holland) | 31

After the Holy Scriptures, I exhort the students to read the Commentaries of Calvin . . . I tell them that he is incomparable in the interpretation of Scripture; and that his Commentaries ought to be held in greater estimation than all that is delivered to us in the writings of the ancient Christian Fathers; so that, in a certain eminent spirit of prophecy, I give the pre-eminence to him beyond most others, indeed beyond them all. I add, that, with regard to what belongs to common places, his Institutes must be read after the Catechism, as a more ample interpretation. But to all this I subjoin the remark, that they must be perused with cautious choice, like all other human compositions."

—JACOBUS ARMINIUS[1]

1. Arminius, *Praestantium ac Eruditorum Virorum Epistolae Ecclesiasticae et Theologicae*, 236–237.

Foreword

FOUR CENTURIES LATER, WHAT are we to make of the rebellion of Jacob Arminius against the Calvinist orthodoxy as taught in sixteenth and seventeenth-century Holland? Should he and the Remonstrants who advocated for his views be valorized 1) as a return to the true intentions of Luther and Calvin, 2) as respecting a proper mystery surrounding the central doctrines of faith and salvation, and 3) for resisting the privileging of causal logic to deform the gospel of grace by framing it within a logically necessary primordial mechanism? Or should we censure Arminius for foolishly selling off the great Reformation treasure of salvation by God's sovereign grace alone and returning to Rome's halfway religion of a faith-plus-works synergy? Certainly, as Dr. Knox's investigations report, Arminius' views led many of his contemporaries to doubt his loyalty to the Protestant cause at the vulnerable historical moment when the Netherlands had shaken off the colonial rule of Spain with its linkage to Roman Catholic doctrine and hierarchical authority.

Readers of Arminius' self-defense should pause to consider that such a powerful attempt at self-correction was attempted from within the heart of the Reformed tradition by someone taught directly by Calvin's own students and younger colleagues, including Beza himself. Hence, Arminius writes his defense in a fraternal spirit, yet as one genuinely alarmed at seemingly inflexible opponents who have allowed their fears to distort the process of doctrinal analysis. In response, Arminius urgently calls the Reformed church to seek honest discussion towards reconciliation, not wishing "dominion over the faith of another man but seeking to increase knowledge, truth piety peace and joy in Christ." Yet, we also see an Arminius inconsistent in the heat of controversy, who can accuse his opponents of the worst of motives, the effect of which made reconciliation much less likely.

To his credit, Arminius engaged in these conversations and debates with an honest sense of the difference between truth and our grasp of truth. Surely a recurrent problem theology struggles with is a kind of *nominalism*—that is, a way of regarding concepts as identical to their referents, as if our conceptual formulations of the truth are equivalent to the truth itself as it is in Jesus Christ. But at its best, theology serves the church not by pointing to its own concepts as encapsulating the reality of God, but rather by using concepts as signposts, pointing towards the living God to whom we seek to bear faithful witness. Arminius seems to have grasped this in a way his opponents unfortunately did not.

In regards to the central issue of predestination itself, it is further to his credit that Arminius had an intuitive sense that predestination and reprobation ought never be seen as belonging together in a kind of equivalence. While the notion of equivalence is not absent in Calvin,[1] he also wrote more than once that the purpose of light is never to blind but to enlighten; to bring life, not to destroy it. If anyone is condemned by Christ, this can only be regarded as "accidental," as when a light shines, it also casts a shadow.[2]

If we could put our finger on the Calvinist misstep, it might point to the abstraction of election as a theme apart from the living agency of the Father's Son, who took upon himself human flesh—not to condemn the world but to save it (John 3:17). To knit together predestination and reprobation as equal bearers of divine glory creates serious confusion at the heart of Christian theology.

---

1. Calvin, *Institutes*, III, XXII, 11.

2. Calvin, *Commentary on John*, Vol. 1, comments on 3:17 (75–76) and 9:39 (254). Also, Vol. 2, 12:40 (47), 12:47 (53), and 20:23 (208).

It presumes that God's will can or ought to to be seen as primary while God's love and mercy are secondary consequences or arbitrary choices. C. S. Lewis has noted how this created for the second generation of Reformers very dark answers to the question of how we are to think of those who have not responded to God's gracious invitation. By raising God's sovereign will to choose as the primary divine attribute, it depicts God as willing to have eternally hated some as to have loved others. That grim portrayal is why in its victory over Arminius the older Protestant orthodoxy helped dig its own grave, albeit unintentionally, for the Enlightenment culture which followed was unable to grasp the original power of the doctrine, finding it either cruel or absurd.[3]

However, a critical question must also be addressed to Arminius and the Remonstrants. Did their solution—to ground the doctrine of predestination upon divine foreknowledge—really resolve Calvinism's dilemma? Or did it lead to obscuring the real significance of the doctrine and give human agency an unfortunate center stage? Did it not replace the electing God with electing man? Or, in the language of modern American evangelicals, did not our decision for Christ increasingly eclipse God's decision for us as the focus of preaching? In retrospect, did either Arminius or his opponents truly find a way to recover and represent the biblical significance of election?

But the story did not end with Arminius. He was just the beginning of Reformed orthodoxy's attempts at self-correction. In the years that followed, another historic seat of Reformed orthodoxy—Scotland, would become the scene of fierce controversies to which names such as Thomas Boston, Samuel Rutherford, and John McCleod Campbell all testify, with Campbell being deposed from the ministry of the Church of Scotland in 1831. It seems then that while the Reformed tradition has a remarkable capacity for being self-critical, it has lacked the ability to reach consensus on reform. The centuries leading to our present moment have seen too many divisions, especially in the United

---

3. Lewis, *English Literature in the Sixteenth Century*, 34. Also, Barth, *Church Dogmatics*, Vol. 2, Part 2, 70.

FOREWORD

States where separation and the withdrawal from association has become a mark of true piety.

These historic controversies still matter today because Arminius remains a favorite target for a newly assertive Calvinism. But rather than engage in a further round of theological pugilism, Dr. Knox's goal is not to argue for some kind of victory, but to get to the heart of Arminius, or to change the metaphor, to sift carefully the wheat from the chaff of his arguments, to honestly acknowledge both strengths and weaknesses. Hopefully, these essays will contribute to an emerging conversation within the Reformed family, one marked by careful listening to the intentions of a theologian's heart in the midst of a historic debate. I would argue that only such an approach can prepare the way for mutual understanding and where appropriate, for a properly repentant rethinking of theological formulations, particularly those which have inadvertently created conceptual control over the truth of the gospel. In offering his readers carefully balanced and scholarly reflections on primary documents, Dr. Knox invites us to set aside rumor and ill-formed opinions in order to engage in fresh conversation with the sources themselves. *Ecclesia semper reformanda est.*

Roger J. Newell
PhD, University of Aberdeen, Scotland
Ordained Minister, the United Reformed Church of England and Wales (1984)
Professor Emeritus of Religious Studies, George Fox University

Preface

I WAS OFFICIALLY INTRODUCED to Pastor-Professor Jacobus Arminius (1560–1609) in my Church History II class at George Fox Seminary in spring of 2001 by one of my favorite professors in graduate school—Dr. Daniel Brunner. For most students, seminary is a shock to the spiritual system as the artificial edifices of denominationalism must give way to hard truths of Scripture and history. As such, I remember Professor Brunner's lecture on Arminius, specifically, because of his suggestion that theologians often make Arminius out to be far more of a doctrinal monster than the Dutch reformer's biblical and Calvinist positions might warrant.

Growing up in several strongly Calvinistic churches, I never heard Arminius spoken about without some disdain or dismissal from my pastors. "Arminianism is not biblical," they would often warn, so my Lutheran professor's opinion shocked me. He even went so far as to call Arminius, "Gracious, loving, humble, but brilliant."[1] I found Brunner's objective presentation intriguing and his challenge to weigh the evidence surrounding Arminius before coming to an absolute conclusion rather persuasive.

Without any personal investigation into the matter, I had assumed for years that Arminianism was heretical, divisive, and doctrinally destructive. Could I have been wrong all this time? Moreover, was I unfairly condemning a man who could be innocent? Was Jacobus Arminius truly to blame for the questionable

---

1. Brunner, "Lecture: Jacob Arminius and the Remonstrants."

(some say heretical) movement named after him? Thus, I sought counsel at seminary, in church, and at home on the matter.

When speaking to a close relative and elder at church, he myopically proclaimed: "Greater minds have already deliberated on this matter (and man) and declared him guilty." When I pressed him for more information, he simply shut down the discussion, shifting to classic Calvinist script that I had heard many times before in church. Yet, despite my affirmation and general agreement with the writings of Jean Calvin, I recall a twinge of guilt regarding my judgment over Arminius.

Therefore, I decided to fully explore the matter of Arminianism vs. Calvinism—and more specifically, I became determined to investigate the man, Arminius, who was simultaneously demonized and lionized in his own time as well as in the present. I had a three-point approach in my investigation: first, I would study the history surrounding Arminius and Arminianism (a given considering I was pursuing a MATS in Christian History and Thought); second, I would explore the theological culture on both sides of the controversy; and finally, I would gather and analyze as many primary sources as possible, in pursuit of the truth.

Fortunately for me, Professor Brunner had referenced some of Arminius' most famous writing, *A Declaration of Sentiments on Predestination*, in class, which provided a wonderful, bountiful resource to begin my research. As in Romans 2:15, I hoped that *A Declaration* would show Arminius' heart regarding the Bible, salvation, predestination, and traditional faith. I was not disappointed, to say the least, as I began to scrutinize Arminius' own words, to see if they could provide insight into his guilt or innocence.

In *A Declaration*, Arminius explains (with both eloquence and enthusiasm) his great disappointment and disagreement with the Supralapsarians under Beza and Gomarus. Although extremely careful in his word-choice regarding his doctrinal positions, based on biblical precedent, he is straightforward, even brusque, in his criticisms of those he considered more political than pious. Though he never penned it, one can almost hear Arminius calling out the Supralapsarians as being Reformed Pharisees and Sadducees who

PREFACE

foolishly and arrogantly considered their own scholarly words and interpretations weightier than the Word of the Lord.

Reading through *A Declaration*, I soon perceived how and why Arminius was considered such a threat (and hero) to so many people around him during that chaotic, political, factional era of faith. His conclusions and admonitions are frequently blunt and forthright, which are necessary in academia. Still, one can also discern Arminius' loving, pastoral approach in *A Declaration*, as he pleads for confession and repentance from those who have taken scripture too far for their own partisan ends.

Thus, at the end of my thesis study, I concluded that Jacobus Arminius was not a vile or devious false teacher; rather, he sought to be, above all things, biblical and Christ-like. Some can (and will) question whether he was truly Calvinist or Reformed, but these ideas are not explicitly in the biblical canon, nor are they necessarily the most important questions to ask.

Ultimately, Arminius spoke and wrote to promote scriptural truths and with reconciliation and true piety in mind, which are universal and historical to the Christian faith. The Supralapsarians had taken Calvin's words and ideas too far in Arminius' learned estimation. They had forgotten the words of Jesus in Matthew 7:1—"Do not judge, or you too will be judged."

In their condemnation of both Catholics and fringe Protestants (who might be guilty of false doctrine), they had neglected the Prophet Isaiah's exhortation in Isaiah 55: "Let the wicked forsake their ways and the unrighteous their thoughts. Let them turn to the Lord, and he will have mercy on them, and to our God for he will freely pardon. For my thoughts are not your thoughts, neither are your ways, my ways, declares the Lord." Redemption—not ruination—is the main goal of God regarding his children on earth.

Nearly twenty years later, I still admire Arminius for his bravery amid his struggles with those hostile, High Calvinist leaders who surrounded and attacked him. Now, having taught Church History and Bible for nearly two decades, I still am favorable of Arminius' approach and explanations (although not always in complete agreement with him in some peripheral areas). Additionally,

Preface

I continue to recommend a healthy and careful scrutiny of Arminius and his most famous work, *A Declaration*, before coming to any absolute conclusions in the matter (and I take the same position with all controversies in Church History).

It is helpful to remember what the Apostle Paul writes in 2 Timothy 2:15: "Do your best to present yourself to God as one approved, a worker who does not need to be ashamed and who *correctly handles the word of truth*." As I say in all my classes, do not fear searching for truth, for God is truth (John 14:6–7) and he wants us to be courageous, honest, hands-on truth sharers in the world—just like Jacobus Arminius.

Acknowledgements

FIRST AND FOREMOST, I offer my sincerest gratitude to my former Church History professor at George Fox University, Dr. Daniel Brunner. While at George Fox Seminary, I had the distinct joy of receiving full and impartial tutelage from Professor Brunner in several history classes, sermons, and guest lectures. Dr. Brunner enlightened our classes without traumatizing us in the sometimes dark and murky world of Church History. My favorite moments were in other Church History classes, when students would ask me how I knew the answer to the professor's question(s), and I would say, "I learned it in Brunner's class." More importantly, he helped students see that we, like all figures in Church History, have a journey and contribution to make to the faith.

Additionally, I appreciate the editorial and proofing assistance of my comrade, former racquetball partner, and local Nampa pastor, Keith Freedman (this is book four for him); former George Fox University student and friend, Heather Harney (this is book five for her); fellow George Fox University/Multnomah University adjunct and soon-to-be-PhD friend, Jenny Matheny; my gifted Liberty University teaching assistant, Deryka Tso; and fellow historian and Liberty professor, Dr. Benjamin Esswein. To one and all, thank you for your savvy editorial suggestions, and for your willingness to read over yet another of my books. You may or may not be happy to know that I have more books to come, soon.

ACKNOWLEDGEMENTS

Finally, because of their generosity and expertise, I am also deeply indebted to both Dr. Roger Newell and President Vic Reasoner for their erudite foreword and afterword contributions. I have had the joy of reading these two scholars' own significant works throughout the years and have grown wiser because of it. Having them add to my study of Arminius is both an honor and a blessing (and I feel confident that Arminius would heartily approve of their inclusion in this investigation of him).

Of course, I could not have completed this book without the on-going support and love of my wife, Brenda, and my very patient sons, Jacob and Joe. This is my fifth book in my academic career, and as with all my literary adventures, their graciousness and kindness to me is both exemplary and inspiring. And yes, sons, I promise to write the sequel to *The Letter of Alon*, very soon.

1

Introduction

ON OCTOBER 30, 1608, Jacobus Arminius presented his *Declaration of Sentiments* to the Assembly of the States of Holland[1] and West Friesland in the Binnenhof[2] at The Hague.[3] This promulgation was offered for two specific purposes. First, Arminius sought to defend himself and his theological views from the spirited attacks of opponents such as Gomarus, Lubbertus, and Plancius. Second, Arminius hoped to bring to light the wrongdoings of the European church and its extremist understanding of certain Christian doctrines.

Having trained in Geneva under Jean Calvin's successor, Theodore Beza (1519–1605), and having further expanded and honed his theology at the University of Leyden[4] from both lectern and the pulpit, Arminius thoroughly presented his theological views in both oral and written form. He spoke in his native Dutch language to an assembly of his peers and religious authorities with the hopes of avoiding a theological rift in Holland—while at the same time hoping to remove a long-standing conflict with the Supralapsarian

1. Also known as The Netherlands.
2. The Binnenhof is the name of the building at The Hague where the Dutch government was housed.
3. The Hague is the seat of government and the administrative center of the Netherlands, on the North Sea coast, capital of the province of South Holland.
4. Also spelled as "Leiden."

faction warring against him. These Supralapsarians espoused "... a confessional and Geneva-oriented dogmatics, high Calvinism with its doctrine of predestination, rigid church discipline, the authority of consistory, classis, and synod, and intolerance of dissent."[5]

Thus, Arminius' *Declaration of Sentiments* is a sophisticated, passionate appeal to reason, scripture, and community.[6] With each section, Arminius seeks not only to demonstrate the error of the attacks on him, but also to point out how and why reconciliation can take place through a careful examination of various precepts of biblical, Christian thought. As Sproul suggests in *Willing to Believe*, Arminius attempted to show that he was not the enemy of Calvinism; in many ways, he was Calvinism's strongest advocate.[7] Furthermore, Arminius wanted his audience to know that, based on both his expressed beliefs and deeds, he was not the false teacher that his adversaries unfairly made him out to be.

With this purpose in mind, *A Declaration of Sentiments on Predestination* contains ten chapters or theses that describe the author's understanding of the predestination of humanity, the providence of God, the freedom of human will, the grace of God, the perseverance of Christians and their assurance of salvation, the possibility of perfection and holiness in the life of the believer, Jesus Christ's divine nature and his part in the justification of humanity before God, and finally, Arminius' own suggested revision of the Dutch confession and the Heidelberg Catechism.[8]

---

5. Bangs, *Arminius*, 54.

6. Arminius' *A Declaration* should not be confused with the *Declaration of Sentiments* composed by Elizabeth Cady Stanton for the first *Woman's Rights Convention* in Seneca Falls, New York, on July 19–20 1848, which outlined a list of complaints against the disenfranchisement of women and provided eleven resolutions arguing for female equality and suffrage.

7. Sproul, *Willing to Believe*, 126.

8. By the request of Elector Frederick III, ruler of the Palatinate (1515–1576), Professor Zacharius Ursinus and preacher Caspar Olevianus (with additional consultation and advice from theology faculty at the University of Heidelberg), wrote a lengthy catechism (eventually fifty-two sections in all) they hoped would unite Protestants over a common understanding of doctrine.

Introduction

With each chapter in *A Declaration*, Arminius carefully built a defense of both his own Christian character and his biblical interpretation through highlighting what he considered to be important errors of hypocritical judgment and shallow hermeneutics in his adversaries. Therefore, the chief goal of this book will be to analyze Arminius' defense of himself and his theology in his *Declaration of Sentiments* against a High Calvinist understanding of theology. Repeatedly, Arminius asserted that he was not diverting from Calvin, Confession, or Catechism; he was merely seeking to follow the truth of God's Word while also hopefully enlightening those in darkness. Substantiating this, Arminius states,

> I here tender my sacred affirmation . . . that, however cogently I may have proved by the most solid (human) arguments any article to be agreeable to the word of God, I will not obtrude it for an article of belief on those of my brethren who may entertain a different opinion respecting it—unless I have plainly proved it from the word of God and have with equal clearness established its truth, and the necessity unto salvation that every Christian should entertain the same belief.[9]

Drawing upon such remarks, excerpts from various primary sources of Arminius' contemporaries and from secondary sources of modern scholarship, and through investigating the cultural milieu and characters surrounding Arminius, an attempt will be made to show how Arminius defended himself in *A Declaration* against numerous Supralapsarian criticisms.

---

9. Arminius, *A Declaration of Sentiments*, 234.

2

The Cultural Surroundings of Arminius and a Declaration

WHEN IT COMES TO history, laypeople may only perceive solitary forces within a historical setting when, in reality, multiple factors are more likely contribute to any one event. Thus, the debate surrounding Arminius may be narrowly and incorrectly defined as a simple disagreement over Calvinist thought when, in fact, the controversy was far more complex considering the culture of Arminius' day. In *The Story of Christianity*, Gonzalez writes, "The sixteenth century had been a period of enormous religious vitality that swept Protestants and Catholics, theologians and rulers, the high and the low."[1] It was during this turbulent period of European history that Arminius lived, studied, and formulated his doctrinal beliefs later to be written down in various documents.

With this in mind, any examination of Arminius' *Declaration of Sentiments* would be incomplete without examining the historical and cultural contexts surrounding its conception. Several key elements were at work in Arminius' life, urging him toward the creation of his *Declaration of Sentiments*. Not the least of these was the presence of the Supralapsarian party in Holland.

---

1. Gonzalez, *The Story of Christianity*, Vol 2, 132.

Although *A Declaration* was produced in response to a specific demand of the Synod of South Holland in Dordrecht, its compilation was long in coming, forged in the civil, social, and theological crucibles surrounding Arminius. By focusing on these specific civil, scholastic, and theological environments that influenced Arminius, a better analysis can be achieved towards understanding how and why *A Declaration* was written.

The Civil Milieu

The civil scene in Arminius' day was complex. Holland had been in a bitter struggle for independence from Spain for many years. During this conflict, the Spanish authorities had executed thousands and banished thousands more Protestants from Holland. Pettegree reports that the Catholic Council of Troubles[2] pronounced 1,100 death sentences and more than 10,000 banishments in just six years.[3] Clearly, it was a brutal and insecure period in history to be living in Holland. Concerning specific Spanish hostilities in Holland, Harrison remarks, "Not only had the Spaniards besieged and taken the little town [Oudewater], they had massacred in cold blood most of its inhabitants."[4]

Arminius was personally affected by this action because this "little town" was the residence of his mother and siblings. In one day, he had lost his entire family. Despite the horror of this event, it was not an uncommon occurence in Europe during the sixteenth-century. Thus, life in the Netherlands was chaotic and unstable; however, in 1558, William of Orange (also known as William the Silent) and his Calvinist forces gained power over the Spanish in controlling most of Holland. In his governance of that territory,

---

2. Also known as the Council of Blood (1567–1574), it was a court established in the Low Countries by the Spanish governor, the Duke of Alba, during the Revolt of the Netherlands to suppress Protestantism and particularism. Alba used the threat of the council to impose the tenth penny, an unpopular tax that united Catholics and Calvinists against Spain. After Alba's departure (1573), the council was abolished.

3. Pettegree, *The Reformation World*, 355.

4. Harrison, *The Beginnings of Arminianism*, 18.

William promoted Calvinist ideals including the synthesis of government and religion.

Despite their efforts, however, it was still a daily struggle against Spanish and Catholic influences attempting to regain control in Holland. Pettegree states, "The relationship between state and church was especially strained in Holland where many town magistrates were of a moderate and non-dogmatic religious stamp."[5] Therefore, when Arminius came upon the Dutch scene as a minister and professor in Amsterdam, those of authority in the government and the Reformed Church were greatly concerned about keeping their country and religion free from Catholic impurities. His moderate position compared to the high Calvinists prompted accusations of dissension and disloyalty—two qualities unacceptable to the power structure in place.

Consequently, in many ways, the rigidity of the Supralapsarians[6] and the Dutch rulers was maintained as a safeguard against the influences that had weakened the stability of the region from previous years. Calvin's theocratic society fit their situation well as it provided a rigid structure for both civil and theological pursuits although the severity of application of Calvinist doctrine issued more from Beza than Calvin. Such high Calvinist leaders, Pettegree says, ". . . hoped to create a godly society in which Calvinism permeated all areas of social life."[7]

Additionally, even though the civil government was ultimately in control rather than the Reformed Church, the Belgic Confession (It is also known as the "Dutch Confession") and the Heidelberg Catechism[8] were utilized in order to provide a check against Catholic thought and influence. A person was a good Christian and Hollander if one were ". . . doctrinally loyal to the

---

5. Pettegree, *The Reformation World*, 357.

6. Supralapsarians hold the position that God first decided that he would save some people and then second, that he would allow sin into the world. By contrast, the infralapsarian ("after the Fall") position is the reverse in that it holds that God first decided who he would allow into the world and second that he would then save people from it.

7. Pettegree, *The Reformation World*, 357.

8. Noll, *Confessions and Catechisms of the Reformation*, 133–136.

Heidelberg Confession as a statement of Calvinism."⁹ Hence, if a minister or leader within the Reformed church failed to comply with either of these two standards, or if they openly disagreed with the doctrines therein, they would immediately be considered heretical, unorthodox, and pro-Catholic subsequently leading to their discharge, or worse. Arminius experienced these labels often in his theological battles at various times in his life.

The Scholastic Milieu

Another factor that should not be ignored is the scholastic aspect of culture and thought in Holland during this period of history. Even though an earlier Reformation style of theological study avoided scholasticism[10] in biblical and doctrinal considerations, many of Arminius' contemporaries slipped back into that practice. Richard Muller states, "Arminius' own writings, in the theological debate leading from the years at the University of Leiden to the Synod of Dort in 1618/9 . . . led to a picture of Arminius as a thinker in virtually total discontinuity with the primary theological and philosophical tendencies of his time."[11] Yet, Arminius was not completely condemned in some theological circles until after his death.

Unfortunately, the result of the re-adoption of this type of thought was the creation of an environment occasionally hypocritical and frequently hostile to theologically inventive or investigative ideas. Gonzalez attests to this when he remarks, "Their [the Supralapsarians] goal was no longer to be entirely open to the Word of God, but rather to uphold and clarify what others had said before them. Dogma was often substituted for faith, and orthodoxy for love."[12] There is also a sense of irony in that Arminius' enemies often accused him of Pelagianism,[13] of over-reliance

9. Bangs, *Arminius*, 107.

10. Scholasticism is the method of study in the Middle Ages that was used to support the doctrines of the church through reason and logic.

11. Muller, "Arminius and the Scholastic Tradition," 263.

12. Gonzalez, *The Story of Christianity*, Vol 2, 133.

13. McGrath, *Historical Theology*, 352.

upon human devices and yet, they elevated their own logical and rational interpretations of doctrine often above what was explicitly stated in Scripture.

Arminius fought against this rigid understanding of doctrine. Like Luther and Calvin before him, he had no trouble leaving some doctrinal elements a mystery. His adversaries, however, were not so laissez-faire on the subject and went to great extremes to put him and his theology down. Arminius notes in his *Declaration*, "A sinister report, has for a long time been industriously and extensively circulated about me, not only among my own countrymen but also among foreigners."[14] Indeed, such awareness was not the result of an over-active imagination. The Supralapsarians had his removal and the extermination of his theological interpretations as the utmost goals of their crusade.

The Theological Milieu

Religious extremism was quite vogue during Arminius' era in history. Reasoner states, "Calvinists believe in absolute predestination; Arminians believe in conditional predestination."[15] As stated earlier, the delicate situation in Holland nearly mandated authoritarian control of most aspects of society in order to assure stability. It was only natural that this severity would bleed into the religious scene. Like the Catholics before them, the Supralapsarians had so rigidly formulated what it meant to be a Christian that all other interpretations were deemed totally unacceptable.

Concerning this harsh judgment placed on Arminius and his followers, Justo Gonzalez remarks, "But the main purpose of the gathering [also known as the 'Synod of Dordrecht'] was the condemnation of Arminianism, necessary in order to end the strife that was dividing the Netherlands and to secure the support of other Reformed churches."[16] For Arminius, though, this condemnation

---

14. Arminius, *A Declaration of Sentiments*, 6.
15. Reasoner, "Arminius, the Scapegoat of Calvinism," 1.
16. Gonzalez, *The Story of Christianity*, Vol 2, 182.

of his theological beliefs was unwarranted and insupportable with a careful reading of the Bible and the Catechism.

Arminius frequently noted this scriptural weakness and scholastic over-reliance in his adversaries' theological approach. He observed that several Dutch church leaders claimed to be pure Calvinists when, in fact, they often went far beyond Calvin in their conclusions. They also presented interpretations that were based more on naturalistic logic and reason rather than on Scripture. Arminius argued that Supralapsarianism was found neither in early Church creeds, nor in the confessional statements of the Reformed and Protestant Churches.

According to Sell, because of this approach, Arminius found their views ". . . offensive for many reasons."[17] Furthermore, speaking on *A Declaration*, Sell contends, "His [Arminius'] contrary contention is that Supralapsarian predestination is not the foundation of Christianity, of salvation, or of assurance."[18] Arminius strongly believed the Supralapsarians were wrong in their understanding of this particular doctrine. Studebaker adds, "It is more likely . . . that Arminius never shared Beza's extreme view but maintained a consistent theological perspective throughout his life."[19]

In the eyes of many of his contemporaries, however, Arminius was extremely obstinate in his judgment of their interpretation and enforcement of doctrine. Statements like, "I am of the opinion, that this doctrine of theirs [the Supralapsarians] contains many things that are both false and impertinent, and at an utter disagreement with each other,"[20] only fueled the fire of their anger against him. Interestingly, such statements also earned Arminius the support and loyalty of many people near him. Thus, "Some proclaim Arminius as a hero. Others denounce him as a heretic."[21] No doubt this dynamic of judgments of Arminius is a direct result of the complexity of times during which he lived.

17. Sell, *The Great Debate*, 9.
18. Ibid., 8.
19. Studebaker, "Theological Influences on the Church," 6.
20. Arminius, *A Declaration of Sentiments*, 69.
21. Cameron, "Arminius—Hero or Heretic?" 213.

Whatever labels Arminius might deserve, though, for certain the manifestations of civil, scholastic, and theological cultures greatly impacted his life. It was within these environments that Arminius interacted with numerous people on both sides of the conflict and formulated his understanding of Reformed theology. In the following chapter, several influential characters in the life of Arminius will be studied, providing an even deeper understanding of the relationship between Arminius, *A Declaration*, and the Supralapsarians.

TIMELINE

1517	Luther's 95 Theses
1529	"Protestantism" coined
1536	Calvin's Institutes
1545	Council of Trent
1559	Birth of Jacob Arminius
1563	Heidelberg Catechism
1564	Death of Jean Calvin
1575	Arminius' mother dies by Council of Blood
1587	Arminius moves to Amsterdam
1588	Arminius becomes pastor Reformed Church
1590	Death of Dirck Koornhert
1590	Arminius married Lijsbet Reael
1603	Arminius begins teaching at Leiden
1603	Arminius' first debate with Gomarus
1605	Death of Theodore Beza
1608	Arminius writes *Declaration of Sentiments*
1608	Arminius defense at The Hague
1609	Death of Arminius
1610	Remonstrants Five Articles
1618	Synod of Dordt (TULIP)
1621	Simon Episcopius writes *Confessio*
1625	Death of Maurice of Orange
1643	Death of Simon Episcopius
1646	Westminster Confession composed
1765	Wesley writes "What is an Arminian?"
1766	Wesley *Plain Account of Christian Perfection*
1795	Remonstrants official recognition as Church

© John S. Knox, 2018

3

Principal Characters in the Development of a Declaration

THE PRECEDING CHAPTER EXAMINED the broad historical, political, and theological factors surrounding Arminius and *A Declaration of Sentiments*. Arminius lived in a period of social complexity that clearly influenced both the motivation and transmission of his presentation. Yet, just as a drama or play is more than the props or the stage setup, so also are the circumstances engulfing Arminius greater than mere historical or cultural matters.

Thus, this chapter will turn its investigation to the people involved in Arminius' life and times (both positively and negatively) in order to aid in a deeper analysis of Arminius and his work. These are the church or institutional leaders that Arminius alluded to (or specifically named) in *A Declaration* who either supported his position or whom he claimed had an incorrect understanding of doctrine and Calvinism. It would be impossible, of course, to investigate every influential individual in Arminius' life. Therefore, an attempt to will be made simply to highlight the people with a vested, personal interest in *A Declaration* in order to show the defining factors between Arminius and the Supralapsarians.

The Life of Jacobus Arminius

It may sound obvious, but the chief character involved in the development of *A Declaration* is its author, Jacobus Arminius. Therefore, with such a pivotal role, it would be beneficial to take a brief look at who he was and how he came to be. This will not be an exhaustive study, though, but more of a summary of his life.[1]

Arminius[2] was born in 1560 in Oudewater, South Holland. Originally, his name was James Hermanns, but after the death of his father and following the fashionable pattern of other "eminent men,"[3] he changed it to the Latinized version, "Arminius."

Once widowed, his mother struggled to provide for her three children and so Arminius was allowed to be adopted by a parish priest named Theodore Aemilius who had converted to Protestantism. This was Arminius' first encounter with Reformed doctrine, but according to Guthrie's account, Aemilius noted that his newly adopted son had ". . . evident marks of an excellent and piously inclined disposition."[4] Sensing the importance and opportunity for his ward, Aemilius enrolled him at a school in Utrecht where he grew in piety and knowledge, much to the delight of his adoptive father.

Sadly, once again tragedy struck as Aemilius unexpectedly died when Arminius was a teenager. Adding to this sorrow was the death of his mother and siblings at the hands of the Spaniards in 1575.[5] Studebaker states, "Spanish troops, seeking to quell the rising independence movement led by William of Orange, attacked Arminius' hometown of Oudewater and savagely killed most of its residents, including his family."[6]

---

1. Despite a resurgence of interest in Jacobus Arminius, there are only a few detailed biographies on the man such as John Guthrie's translation of Remonstrant Minister Caspar Brandt's *The Life of James Arminius* (1857), A.W. Harrison's *The Beginning of Arminianism* (1926), and Carl Bangs' *Arminius* (1971).
2. He is also referred to as "James."
3. Guthrie, *The Life of James Arminius*, 33–34.
4. Ibid., 36.
5. See chapter two for more details regarding the Spanish Conflict.
6. Studebaker, "Theological Influences on the Church," 5.

Despite this sorrowful situation, Arminius was able to procure a secure home with a new patron named Rudolph Snellius—a proficient linguist and mathematician who offered young Arminius yet another opportunity to learn and study. Eventually, when he reached a proper age, Arminius began attending the new University at Leyden. At the same time, he roomed with Peter Bertius, Sr., pastor of a local Reformed Church at Rotterdam. His studies lasted from 1576–1582 and during this time, he was sent to Geneva to cultivate his training in the ways of orthodox Protestantism.

In Geneva, Arminius fortuitously studied under Theodore Beza—John Calvin's heir apparent and official standard-bearer for the Calvinist faith. He became well versed in the High Calvinist ways of Beza and his fellow Supralapsarians. Despite their "indoctrination" of the young scholar, Arminius nevertheless found much of Beza's conclusions on Calvinist thought and doctrine to be spurious and unacceptable.[7] This eventually would cause a great deal of consternation on the part of the advocates of high Calvinism, but it did not keep Arminius from obtaining a ministerial position.

In 1587, Arminius moved to Amsterdam and began the protocol of meetings, oral examinations, and trial-preaching necessary before becoming ordained as a minister in the Dutch Reformed Church. Despite some tense moments, Arminius was finally admitted as minister of the Church in Amsterdam in 1588. Immediately after beginning his official position, he was called upon to contest and disprove the "liberal" views of Dirck Koornhert, a popular theologian.

Koornhert was a lay theologian who first had been secretary of State and then later worked on a Dutch translation of Erasmus' Latin New Testament.[8] He also had publicly challenged the rigid Supralapsarian understanding of predestination and promoted a more tolerant, humanist understanding of doctrine. Arminius' superiors hoped he would champion the views of High Calvinism; instead, he ended up agreeing with Koornhert's interpretation

7. Olson, *The Story of Christian Theology*, 456.
8. Harrison, *The Beginnings of Arminianism*, 25.

of Scripture—at least concerning predestination. This newfound understanding of doctrine and predestination eventually spilled into Arminius' preaching duties and he found himself the center and focus of intense debate. Thereafter, he was accused of several heresies, from Pelagianism[9] to Arianism to Socinianism.[10]

According to his critics, Arminius was Pelagian because of his disagreement with the irresistibility of the Holy Spirit and was Socinian because he doubted that God would elect anyone to damnation. Drawing upon his personal talent for scholarship, Arminius employed reason and authority to defend his positions.[11] Furthermore, he put a low priority on the doctrinal statements of his theological peers that seemed beyond scriptural confirmation because, as maintained by Harrison,

> All his theology was Biblical, Arminius would assert. He allowed no rival authority in the realm of faith. The views of the fathers and the decrees of the Church Councils were important; the fundamental axioms and intuitions of the human mind were very potent; but at the best their authority was secondary, while that of the Scriptures was all in all.[12]

Even though his approach caused some people to become apoplectic, Arminius still was a very popular speaker and teacher. Reasoner writes, "Arminius had the reputation of being a brilliant preacher, a gifted Bible exegete, and a humble and dedicated Christian. His expositional preaching drew large crowds."[13] This popularity, combined with his resistance to Supralapsarianism, made Arminius a real threat to the Calvinist camp in Leyden and Geneva.

---

9. Named after a monk in the fifth century, CE, Pelagianism asserts that Adam's original sin was not passed on to all generations of humanity. Thus, somewhat like in Islam, people are born innocent, free from sin, and then proceed (potentially but not absolutely) to volitionally choose to do evil.

10. Socianism is a Reformation-era heresy that denied Christ's deity, substitutionary atonement, and God's foreknowledge and foreordination.

11. Harrison, *The Beginnings of Arminianism*, 40.

12. Ibid., 40–41.

13. Reasoner, "Arminius, the Scapegoat of Calvinism," 1.

Jacobus Arminius Stands His Ground

With the devastating outbreak of the Plague in 1602 and the deaths of Leyden professors Franciscus Junius (1545–1602)[14] and Luke Trelcatius (1545–1602), he had an opportunity thrust upon him to teach at the University of Leyden. Before their deaths, many letters and essays had passed between these men and Arminius on doctrinal matters, providing ample ammunition for both advocate and adversary alike concerning Arminius.

In fact, despite being invited by the board of governors at the University to apply, several men also employed there (Gomarus, Cuchlinus,[15] Plancius, Hommius[16]) vehemently fought against his joining the faculty at Leyden. According to "The Personal History of Arminius,"[17] his future adversary, Gomarus, fervently claimed,

> I cannot with good conscience so far dissemble as not to express my apprehensions, that the call of Arminius, for the promoting of which I understand you are now convened, will in my judgment be the cause of most serious injury to the University, on account of the heterodoxy which he maintained . . . in his very grievous dissensions with Junius on the subject of Predestination.[18]

Fortunately for Arminius, the governors of the University felt that Gomarus and his fellow objectors had little proof for substantiating their concerns. Once Arminius had acceptably answered all their questions, without giving them suitable reasons for rejection, they concluded with asking him to accept the professorship

---

14. Franciscus Junius, the Elder, was a Reformation scholar and theologian who studied under both Jean Calvin and Theodore Beza. Franciscus Junius, the Younger, was a scholarly expert in ancient Germanic languages.

15. A Dutch Reformed pastor and Calvinist, Johannes Cuchlinus (1546–1606) was Arminius' uncle by marriage (1596).

16. Festus Hommius (1576–1612) was a pastor in Leiden who "openly accused Arminius of introducing doctrinal innovations." Gunter, *Arminius and His Declaration of Sentiments*, 71.

17. Arminius, "The Personal History of Arminius," *The Works of James Arminius*, 172.

18. Ibid., 185.

at Leyden.[19] This bothered his critics immensely and only initiated further attacks against him.

In 1603, Arminius had his first official debate with Franciscus Gomarus at The Hague. Gomarus again accused him of Pelagianism and of being pro-Catholic,[20] allegations against which Arminius once more successfully defended himself. This would be the beginning of a long and bitter struggle between the two men and their respective theological positions, culminating in creation of *A Declaration of Sentiments* in 1608.

Arminius' Advocates

Unfortunately, in the assessment of most historical controversies, the negative is more often focused upon than the positive. Thus, the information and sketches of those who disagreed with Arminius outweigh those of the persons who agreed with him. Nevertheless, some key figures positively contributing to the promotion of Arminius and his convictions can be observed. Without their active participation in supporting, defending, and promoting Arminius, his impact on the theological world would probably not have been as dramatic.

Theodore Aemilius

The role of local priest Theodore Aemilius in Arminius' life was alluded to earlier in this chapter, but his importance cannot be stressed enough. Although little is known about him, what information is available comes through the testimony of Peter Bertius.[21] Coming to Arminius' aid after the death of his father, Harmen, Aemilius was most likely the "spark" that set Arminius' fire ablaze for theological knowledge.

---

19. Bangs, *Arminius*, 235.
20. Ibid., 304.
21. Ibid., 33.

Studebaker writes, "This priest, Theodore Aemilius, apparently supervised Arminius' early studies in Latin, Greek, and Theology and took the boy into his home in Utrecht. Aemilius died when Arminius was about fourteen."[22] In his oration offered sometime after Arminius' passing, Peter Bertius describes Aemilius as ". . . a person of great honor and respectability"[23] whose ". . . memory is to this day cherished."[24]

Whether he continued to minister at a specific parish while taking care of Arminius is unknown. As a converted Catholic priest to Protestantism—and living in territory not completely Reformed—Theodore may have had trouble finding a rectory to oversee. As Gonzalez remarks,

> The Council of Trent had condemned the views of Luther and Calvin on grace and predestination; but there were many who feared that, in an extreme reaction against Protestantism, this could lead to a denial of St. Augustine's teachings. Thus arose among Catholics a series of controversies over grace and predestination.[25] Despite this theological and political minefield, Aemilius did, however, still manage to provide Arminius with classic academic training as well as the fundamentals of biblical scholarship.[26]

The discipline and thirst for theological knowledge that Arminius displayed throughout his life were clearly cultivated by Theodore in Arminius' early years. As Brian indicates, "Aemilius's impact upon young Arminius cannot be overstated."[27] No doubt, this edifying and beneficial relationship later provided the tools

---

22. Studebaker, "Theological Influences on the Church," 4.
23. Bertius, "An Oration," 17.
24. Ibid.
25. Gonzalez, *The Story of Christianity*, Vol. 2, 214.
26. One also wonders if this might be why Arminius so often cited his agreement with both St. Augustine and traditional Calvinist thought in his *Declaration of Sentiments*.
27. Brian, *Jacob Arminius*, chapter two.

Arminius needed to stand firm amid so many controversial religious storms that surrounded him.

Peter Bertius (The Younger)

Peter Bertius, Jr. (1565–1629) was the son of the pastor at the Reformed Church in Rotterdam. The Bertius family allowed Arminius to live with them as a young man. The younger Peter and Arminius attended the University of Leyden together. Their friendship was life-long[28] and their bond deep and intimate.

Speaking at the memorial for Arminius after his death in 1609, Bertius explained, "I am about to make some observations on the Life and Death of that reverend and incomparable man."[29] He went on to state, "We have just committed... James Arminius, as a real temple of the Holy Spirit, but shaken, and worn down, and broken in pieces, by labours, watchings, contests, diseases, and afflictions."[30] Bertius knew Arminius' struggles in his life because he endured them, too, by his side over the years. He also knew that what made Arminius great was not his popularity, nor his awards and degrees, but his character and conviction.

In recounting Arminius' life and showing his great admiration, Bertius remarked,

> Arminius was born to fame and to glory, with sails full-stretched, prosperous gales, and with his company of rowers in a complete state of efficiency; he had gained the approbation and favour of all who knew him, and to put his modesty and patience to the test by means of the cross and afflictions.[31]

The rest of his oration was dedicated to defending and explaining Arminius' words and deeds. Bertius finished his eulogy, stating, "There lived a man, whom it was not possible, for those

---

28. Harrison, *Arminianism*, 13.
29. Bertius, "An Oration," 14.
30. Ibid., 16.
31. Ibid., 29.

who knew him, sufficiently to esteem; those who entertained no esteem for him, are such as never knew him well enough to appreciate his merits."[32]

Bertius was more than just a colleague of Arminius. He was a true friend and deeply respected him. Bertius' closeness to Arminius gave him insight into his friend's life and provided courage to stand up for him in life, death, and theology. Beyond that, though, he connected with the heart of Arminius. He felt, like Arminius, that many people misunderstood him. Consequently, in his message, Bertius pointed to *A Declaration* and stated,

> He made a noble *Declaration of his Sentiments*, and an excellent profession of his faith, in the presence of many witnesses... So highly did he estimate the prudence and sagacity of that august body, as to hope, in the case of his death, that some of them would not fail to defend, by the patronage of their wisdom and favour, the justice of that cause, which had once been offered to them for examination and approval.[33]

After Arminius's death in 1609, Bertius published a theologically controversial work that took Arminius' theological interpretations even farther, *Hymenaeus Desertor* (1612),[34] which ultimately ended his theological teaching career. However, under King Louis XIII, Bertius was appointed first court cosmographer and later received the title of royal historian.[35]

Johannes Uitenbogaert

Uitenbogaert (1557–1644)[36] was also a close friend of Arminius from his days at the University in Leyden, although they most likely

---

32. Ibid., 47.
33. Ibid., 41.
34. Bertius, *Hymenaeus Desertor*.
35. Goffart, *Historical Atlases*, 70.
36. Also spelled Uytenbogaert or Wtenbogaert.

met while in Geneva.³⁷ Born at Utrecht, he converted to Protestantism in defiance of Catholic authorities. He had considered going to law school, but his conscience urged him to pursue theological studies and ordination in the Reformed school of theology.

He, like Arminius, was a pastor in the Dutch Reformed Church, but he was eventually invited by Prince Maurice to become an official minister in The Hague. This position allowed him great influence in support of his friend, Arminius, and in the promotion of their shared theological beliefs. Later, he became a close friend of Oldenbarnevelt,³⁸ the transitory ruler of the Netherlands.

Many of Arminius' enemies considered him and Uitenbogaert to be of the same mindset and so attacked them—fiercely, openly, and often. In fact, after Arminius' appointment at the University, malicious gossip about Arminius and Uitenbogaert was more than plentiful.³⁹ Stemming from various correspondence, lectures, sermons, and debates, suspicion of Arminius and his cohort grew until the meeting of the Synod of South Holland. In order to assure proper orthodox teaching, the Synod demanded that all ministers had thirty days to tender their statements of belief on the Confession and Catechism to their local presbytery.⁴⁰ This led to Arminius' writing *A Declaration of Sentiments*—a task completed in just ten days.

After the death of Arminius in 1609, "Forty-six advocates of Arminius's theology met in the city of Gouda in 1610 under the leadership of Hans Uytenbogaert (a pastor) and Simon Episcopius."⁴¹ Uitenbogaert took the leadership role of the Arminian party and, along with Arminius' pupil and successor, Simon Episcopius,⁴²

---

37. Bangs, *Arminius*, 36.

38. Oldenbarnevelt was an advisor first to Prince William and later to his son, Maurice. He figured large in the political arena in the five decades that preceded the Synod of Dordt. Although officially he held office in just one of the eleven provinces of the Netherlands, Oldenbarnevelt exercised tremendous influence in all branches of the national government.

39. Bangs, *Arminius*, 292.

40. Ibid., 307.

41. Peterson and Williams, *Why I Am Not an Arminian*, 112.

42. See Mark A. Ellis, *Simon Episcopius' Doctrine of Original Sin* (2006) for

they helped develop the Five Articles of the Remonstrants[43] that were intended to be a systematic summary statement of Arminius' theological doctrines.[44] Many historians and theologians do not believe that they maintained the integrity of Arminius' true values, however. Sell states, "We have observed that in important respects Arminius was not an Arminian."[45] Furthermore, Cameron claims that Arminius "... does not fit easily into the Calvinist-Arminian patterns of theological pigeon-holing."[46]

Unfortunately, it is impossible to know whether Arminius would have supported or promoted Uitenbogaert's synopsis of his beliefs. In many ways, Arminius may have found the extremism of the Remonstrants just as unappealing as that of the Supralapsarians. From his own writings, however, there is no doubt that he would have rejected major issues within the TULIP[47] understanding of Calvinism that was created in direct response to the Remonstrants' five points of doctrine.

---

more information on Arminius's successor.

43. The Remonstrants articles are summarized as follows: 1. God has decreed to save through Jesus Christ those of the fallen and sinful race who through the grace of the Holy Spirit believe in him, but leaves in sin the incorrigible and unbelieving. 2. Christ died for all humanity (not just for the elect), but no one except the believer has remission of sin. 3. Man or Woman can neither of themselves nor of their free will do anything truly good until they are born again of God, in Christ, through the Holy Spirit. 4. All good deeds or movements in the regenerate must be ascribed to the grace of God but his grace is not irresistible. 5.Those who are incorporated into Christ by a true faith have power given them through the assisting grace of the Holy Spirit to persevere in the faith. But it is possible for a believer to fall from grace.

44. Lutzer, *The Doctrines That Divide*, 178.

45. Sell, *The Great Debate*, 97.

46. Cameron, "Arminius—Hero or Heretic?" 227.

47. The traditional five points of Calvinism (associated with the acronym, "TULIP") was commissioned by the Dutch Reformed Church and composed during the Synod of Dordt (1618–1619), which met in Dordrecht, South Holland. The religious assembly penned eighteen articles on proper Reformed doctrine that can be condensed to five main ideas, which challenged the five theological assertions of the Remonstrants. TULIP stands for total depravity, unconditional election, limited atonement, irresistible grace, and the perseverance of the saints.

CHARACTERS IN THE DEVELOPMENT OF A DECLARATION

Arminius' Adversaries

As mentioned earlier, it is important to maintain scholarly balance in this subject. Therefore, although there may be more members of the anti-Arminius camp, only four will follow: Calvin, Beza, Gomarus, and Plancius. Either directly or indirectly, each one of these reformed leaders influenced Arminius' life and efforts.

Jean Calvin

It may seem preposterous to accuse Jean [John] Calvin of being an adversary of Arminius considering he died in 1564 when Arminius was only four years old (and considering that the word and/or idea of "Supralapsarian" had not been specificall espoused, yet). However, the further development of some of Calvin's doctrinal beliefs were problematic for Arminius, and Calvin's theocratic understanding of government and religion created a backdrop in Europe that would affect Arminius' entire life—often negatively.

Ironically, though, Calvin's *Institutes of Religion*[48] was highly praised by Arminius. According to Cameron, Arminius considered the *Institutes* "... more to be valued than anything that is handed down to us in the writings of the Fathers."[49] Furthermore, reading through Arminius' *Declaration*, it is simple enough to find reference after reference that agrees with and displays proper Calvinist thought.

Yet, there are key aspects that Arminius disagreed with such as the notion of double election or double predestination. In Arminius' mind, if God made some human beings repentant and others rebellious, that would make God the author of sin—an idea contradicting the belief of a loving God. As Pinnock and Wagner

---

48. Calvin, *Institutes of the Christian Religion* (1536). Originally one book, it evolved into four books on proper Protestant doctrine concerning God the Creator, redemption mediated through Christ, appropriation of redemption, and the church's relationship to greater society. In an attempt to provide assurance or confidence in one's salvation, Calvin elaborated on why people believe in the Christian, biblical message or not—thus, focusing on the doctrine of Predestination.

49. Bangs, "Arminius as a Reformed Theologian," 216.

note, "Though Arminius differed with Calvin on predestination, Arminius was, and believed he was, consistently Reformed."[50]

The adversarial aspects of the legacy of Calvin can further be seen in the theocracy at work in Geneva and Amsterdam as well as the rigid administration and promotion of doctrine. In Geneva, Calvin and his followers attempted to blend religion and government. With this as a foundation, they used the Bible to enforce a strict, morally conservative civil scene with harsh penalties and punishments for the offender.[51] Furthermore, Calvinism in Geneva adhered to a rigid understanding of doctrine that did not tolerate dissension. In many ways, it was the same in Amsterdam.

The consequences of such practices are deserving of another book, but suffice it to say that Arminius' life would have been less troubled without the intrusion of the state in theological matters of discussion. Holland, like Geneva, held Calvin up as a great theological "guru," but the interpretation and application of his writings sometimes went beyond what was explicitly expressed in Scripture. Bangs writes,

> The modern approach would be to compare the doctrinal statements of Arminius with those of Calvin. The result would be a mixture of aggreement and dissent, with possibly no less agreement or more dissent than would be found in many later Calvinists, expecially those of our time. But in Holland in Arminius' time, Calvin was not the centreal point of reference. He had receded into the recent past.[52]

Thus, for Arminius and others, the Supralapsarians were presuming far too much authority in doctrinal and biblical matters. Reasoner remarks, "Beza had made the Calvinistic position more rigid and had taught Supralapsarianism—that the decrees of election and damnation came prior to the decree to create man."[53] Furthermore, their responses to dissent and dialogue was far from

---

50. Pinnock and Wagner, *Grace for All*, 157.
51. Olson, *The Story of Christian Theology*, 410.
52. Bangs, "Arminius as a Reformed Theologian," 216.
53. Reasoner, "Arminius, the Scapegoat of Calvinism," 1.

the biblical injuction to "restore each other gently" (Galatians 6:1). Thus, Arminius found this situation improper, ill-advised, and needing reprovement or repair.

Theodore Beza

Theodore Beza, Calvin's successor (and his son-in-law), carried on Calvin's work after his death, but in a differing fashion (based in part on the scholary ideas of Jerome Zanchius [1516–1590] and others). Attesting to this, Bray states, "There is clear evidence that in some areas Beza did, in fact, alter the practice and the teaching of Calvin. The alterations of Beza are especially striking in the field of government."[54] Many found this new twist on Calvinism too rigid and thus, inappropriate; "Arminius faced a crisis of conscience and he responded with integrity."[55]

Arminius disagreed with much of Beza's interpretation of Calvin and the Bible, but Beza did not care much for Arminius' approach either. Bangs notes in correspondence between the two, "Beza commends Arminius for his ability and diligence, but not for his theology . . . . Arminius likewise praises Beza for a wonderful mind which is worthy of a student's emulation. Nothing about predestination."[56] They evidently were on different sides of the theological spectrum both in doctrine and style leading them to reserved remarks about each other. Eventually, Arminius found Beza's Supralapsarianism to be intolerable—so intolerable that Arminius refused to ". . . capitulate to the pressures of Beza and his disciples in Holland."[57]

This Supralapsarian pressure was real and sustained. Those in Beza's camp reported back to him regularly of the heresies and faulty theological thought that Arminius was spreading. Beza would then work in the political and theological arena to thwart

---

54. Bray, *Theodore Beza's Doctrine of Predestination*, 9.
55. Reasoner, "Arminius, the Scapegoat of Calvinism," 1.
56. Bangs, *Arminius*, 75.
57. Ibid., 198.

Arminius' efforts in order to bolster the Supralapsarians' attempts at crushing this "weak" theology. In fact, Bangs notes, "After his death, he became a byword for heresy in Reformed and Lutheran circles. His name became attached to schools of theology as diverse as Dutch Remonstrantism, Anglican high churchmanship, Wesleyan revivalism, and New England liberal Puritanism."[58]

Franciscus Gomarus

Born in Bruges, Flanders, one year before Jean Calvin's death (1563), Franciscus Gomarus and his siblings grew up with parents that followed Reformed thought. A precocious lad, Gomarus pursued a classical education wherein he began his studies of theology, philosophy, rhetoric, and the law.

Like many other Protestants of the time, in 1577, the Gomarus family was forced to flee eastward to Germany because of extremist Catholic and Lutheran oppression. In Strasbourg, Germany, Gomarus began his classical studies under staunch Calvinists like Johann Sturm, a German educator and advisor (1507–1589).[59]

When more religious persecution and oppressive measures were instituted, Gomarus moved again to Neustadt, where he received tutelage from Supralapsarian professors Zacharias Ursinus (formerly at the University of Heidelberg) and Hieronymus Zanchius (at the Casmirianum Academy). In 1582, he traveled to England to take some courses at Oxford University, but he finally graduated in 1584 from the University of Cambridge. He received his doctoral degree from the University of Heidelberg in 1594.

Based on available historical evidence, it is safe to say that Gomarus was Arminius' chief theological rival. From the moment Arminius considered joining the faculty at the University of Leyden,

---

58. Bangs, "Arminius as a Reformed Theologian," 209.

59. More than just a strict Calvinist, Johann Sturm was also active in pedagogical studies, including curriculum development combining Reformation and Humanist ideals. He promoted grammar, rhetoric, Ciceronian dialectic, and rote memorization in his educational model to help students hone skills of neutral hermeneutics.

Gomarus seemed to make it his responsibility to prevent Arminius from teaching there and from spreading his brand of theology. He felt Arminius should not be in that position of influence in the theological sphere because his theology was "too Pelagian."

In no uncertain terms, Gomarus let the governors know he did not want Arminius appointed; however, after Arminius had been hired over the objections of Gomarus, the latter then doggedly criticized, confronted, and debated with Arminius every chance that he could. He became essentially what Bangs calls an "agent of hostility to Arminius."[60] Observing the active aggression of Gomarus, it is easy to conclude that he was simply a bitter man; however, many would disagree with this hasty conclusion.

In *Portraits of Faithful Saints*, Hanko sees Gomarus as a man who was a "staunch defender of the faith" and one who "stood for the truth;" however, many thought Gomarus to be " . . . obnoxious at times and barely tolerable."[61] Either way, Arminius avoided the conflict when he could, but eight years later, he finally stood against Gomarus in front of the Assembly to determine if his Declaration or Gomarus' position was correct.

Just as Arminius had provided a full and detailed explanation of the realities and biblical foundation of predestination and freedom of human will, Gomarus presented a thirty-two-part treatise on proper Reformed doctrine entitled, "Of God's Predestination."[62] Perhaps he hoped to sway his audience with a tidal wave of evidence to refute a substantial foe. As Hanko states, "His opponent, Jacobus Arminius, popular with students and ministers, gracious, kind, tolerant, filled with concern for friend and foe alike, presents quite a contrast. But Arminius was the heretic, and Gomarus stood for the truth."[63].

---

60. Bangs, *Arminius*, 235.
61. Hanko, *Portraits of Faithful Saints*, part three.
62. From *Works of Arminius*, Vol 3, 521–658.
63. Hanko, *Portraits of Faithful Saints*, part three.

In his response to Arminius' defense of his theology, Gomarus clearly states in Chapter XIII,

> Therefore, also, the object of predestination to its own ends—to speak accurately and without prolepsis (which, when used in this argument, begets obscurity)—are rational creatures, not as actually about to be saved or lost, to be created, about to fall or stand fast, or about to be restored; but, so far as remote and indefinite ability goes, savable, damnable, creable [creatable], liable to fall, restorable. And that is proved, beyond controversy, by the nature and order of the object and of the cause both efficient and final. For the object, in the order of nature, precedes the operation of the power attached to it and occupied about it, and therefore also the object of predestination precedes predestination itself; nay, and exceeds it in extent also, as we have shown (in Thesis X): but being about to be saved, to be created, to fall, to be restored, does not exceed nor precede predestination, but follows it: Therefore, it is not the object of it. For, as the creable depends on the indeterminate and absolute omnipotence of God, so what is to be created depends on that omnipotence determined to creation by predestination of the will; and therefore, cannot come before predestination, which is its efficient cause.

The end result was not what Gomarus had hoped to occur. He wanted Arminius and his theology to be rejected once and for all. Instead, Arminius found an audience willing to listen to his courteous and soft-spoken interpretation of doctrine. Gomarus' attack had backfired. As indicated by Bangs, the Assembly members were "... offended by Gomarus' speech" and "... could not believe [Arminius] to be the two-faced person Gomarus pictured him to be."[64]

Despite this setback, Gomarus immediately re-challenged Arminius to another debate sometime during the next year. However, it was never to occur because Arminius died soon thereafter in 1609. Due to the violence that followed because of riots in several Dutch cities over the Remonstrants, Gomarus and the other

---

64. Bangs, *Arminius*, 320.

Supralapsarians found the Synod of 1618 more easily swayed in denouncing Arminius' teachings as depicted in the Remonstrants' five points.

According to Olson, with the support of Prince Maurice of Nassau, the Synod "... concluded by condemning as heretics the Remonstrant leaders."[65] This resulted in hundreds of ministers, teachers, and theologians in support of the Arminian party being removed from their respective positions and subsequently sent into exile or imprisoned.

Franciscus Gomarus had finally conquered Arminius and his theology—at least for the moment. However, Arminianism arose to become an important theological movement in Europe and the West, but no such large movement of "Gomarians" sprung forth from his efforts to extinguish the dangerous theology of his most dangerous opponent—Jacobus Arminius.

Petrus Plancius

Gomarus was not alone in his condemnation of Arminius. In fact, clergyman and astronomer Petrus Plancius was considered by many to be the "first great antagonist of Arminius"[66] living in Holland. Although known more for his involvement in the founding of the Dutch East India Company and his famous map, "Nova et exacta Terrarum Tabula geographica et hydrographica,"[67] Gunter writes that Plancius "... would prove to be for many years a thorn in the side of Arminius."[68] Owing to his advocacy and total commitment to the high Calvinist understanding of doctrine, Petrus was considered by many Hollanders to be "not a mild Calvinist."[69] Thus, he and Arminius vehemently disagreed on the validity of Supralapsarian doctrinal understandings.

---

65. Olson *The Story of Christian Theology*, 463.
66. Bangs, *Arminius*, 107.
67. Matei-Chesnoiu, *Re-imagining Western European Geography*, 174.
68. Gunter, *Arminius and His Declaration of Sentiments*, 50.
69. Ibid., 117.

Plancius, like Arminius, suffered under Spanish and Catholic rule in West Flanders. He also, like Arminius, was a minister in the Dutch Reformed Church. Beyond that, however, they had very little in common. Bangs describes him as having "bitter enmity toward Arminius"[70] and that he ". . . was forceful, and many were to feel his force"[71]—including Arminius.

Plancius frequently made accusations of heresy against Arminius and his fellow-thinkers. He kept a ". . . running attack on Arminius and his friends, calling them Coornhertians, Neo-Pelagians, and the like."[72] His approach was less than courteous or professional. In fact, he was rather conniving in his efforts to make Arminius look bad. He would frequently work in tandem with Gomarus or Lubbertus[73] in schemes to bring Arminius' bad theology out into the open for judgment. Fortunately for Arminius, he was able to defend himself against this man's hostility.

These men, on both sides of the issue, were integral in the life of Arminius, and each either subtly or overtly helped mold his understanding of theology as expressed in *A Declaration*. It is interesting to consider what would have occurred had one or more of them been absent in Arminius' life. Often, human beings only act because of the catalysts in their environment. Arminius' own response to the culture surrounding him and the people in his life (and his *Declaration of Sentiments*) will be examined in the next chapter.

---

70. Ibid., 119.

71. Ibid.

72. Ibid., 272.

73. Sigrandus Lubbertus (1556–1625) was a professor at the University of Franeker who upheld the Supralapsarian doctrine (Beza was one of his former professors in Geneva). He was deeply involved in the Synod of Dort (1618–1619) and was a chief opponent of Arminianism and Socianism.

CHARACTERS IN THE DEVELOPMENT OF A DECLARATION

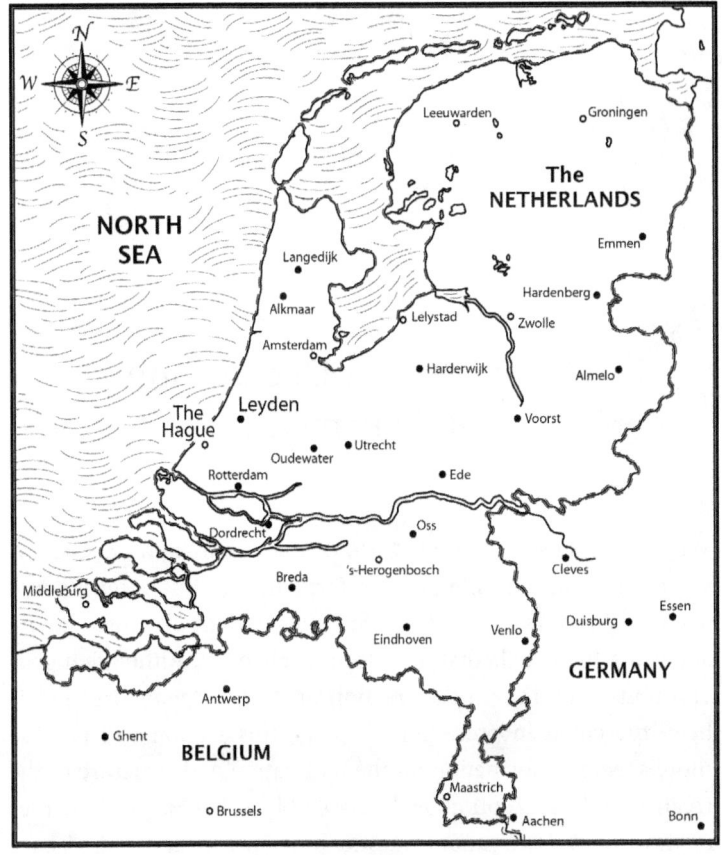

© John S. Knox, 2018

4

Overview of a Declaration of Sentiments

WITH A FULLER UNDERSTANDING of the culture and persons involved in Arminius' life and the formation of his *Declaration of Sentiments*, an overview of this document will be presented before analyzing the details that lie within its chapters. Although a general understanding on the creation of *A Declaration* already has been presented in preceding chapters, this section will provide more specific information on the motivation and structure of the treatise, and its reception by the Assembly at The Hague. In earlier analysis of *A Declaration*, questions of "when" and "who" have been addressed. Now, attention will be turned to the "why" questions concerning Arminius and his document of defense.

A Declaration is not especially long (originally seventy pages), nor is it overly verbose. As such, Arminius had a very clear purpose in creating it. It was written first as a challenge to high Calvinist attacks and second as a message of biblical truth according to Arminius. Many scholars applaud the simple elegance of its message although just as many consider its significance and motivation questionable. In approval, Godfrey states, "Arminius wrote his 'Declaration of Sentiments,' [it is] probably the best summary of his beliefs. Arminius had been insisting that he was only trying to protect the church from the extremes of Calvinism, especially Supralapsarianism."[1]

Countering this positive appraisal, Bloesch writes,

> Perhaps the most subtle form of works-righteousness is faith-moralism, in which lip service is paid to the doctrine of justification by faith, but faith is seen as a human work or virtue... Arminius opened the door to faith-moralism by regarding faith as the first cause of justification, not the instrument by which man accepts justification.[2]

These scholars, like countless others, would likely agree that Arminius' writings and theology were often profound, though not necessarily correct in their final judgments. The following chapter will deal with the controversy over Arminius' theological defense more fully, but suffice it to say that, at the very least, *A Declaration of Sentiments* is a well-written, high-profile treatise[3] that sufficiently served Arminius in his time of need.

Standing before a mixed assembly of advocates, friends, hostile and fearful lords, theologians, and ministers, Arminius sought not only to defend himself against his attackers, but he hoped also to enlighten and calm his peers and judges, alike. He was not merely attempting to vanquish his enemies; he also hoped to save them from theological misconceptions that he considered to be "... in contradiction either to the Word of God, or the Confession of the Belgic Churches."[4] Thus, in his presentation, he devoted ten chapters toward this pursuit of clear, biblically sound thinking.

Arminius began his treatise with an explanation of his presence before the assembly. It is in these few pages that the reader encounters his expressed frustration and his account of the suffering that he has experienced in the years leading up to what Bangs calls the Dutch "Inquisition."[5] He recounted the attacks against him,

1. Godfrey, "Who Was Arminius?"
2. Bloesch, *Essentials of Evangelical Theology*, 60.
3. Harrison, *The Beginnings of Arminianism*, 108.
4. Arminius, *A Declaration of Sentiments*, 49.
5. Bangs, *Arminius*, 307.

both overt and surreptitious, as well as the manipulation of facts and numerous personal petty challenges made by his colleagues—all unjust and unnecessary in his opinion.

In this initial address, he remarked, "I find by experience that this distorted version of the matter has procured for me not a few proofs of hatred and ill-will from many persons."[6] This theme will be repeated time and time again throughout the rest of *A Declaration*. In it, Arminius suggests that a distortion of truth is the cause of the conflict that surrounded him, but the distortion is not his; rather, it originated from his Supralapsarian attackers.

He pled for fairness from his judges as to whether he had actually perverted the truth of Scripture and doctrine. He assured them that he would accept their punishment if they rejected his *Declaration of Sentiments* and the theological understandings it presented. However, he also hoped that they would acquit him and come to his aid if they found his beliefs in keeping with the Confession and the Bible.

As mentioned earlier, one of the biggest complaints from Gomarus and his Supralapsarian Amsterdam camp was that Arminius had rejected God's doctrine of predestination of both saint and sinner as taught by Calvin. Arminius had long struggled against the doctrine of Supralapsarianism. He knew it was the cornerstone of his opponents' argument against him and was their "primary item of contention."[7]

With this knowledge, he began Section I of *A Declaration* with the statement, "The first and most important article in Religion on which I have to offer my views, and which for many years past has engaged my attention, is the Predestination of God, that is, the Election of men to salvation, and the Reprobation of them to destruction."[8] This statement may be succinct, but the rest of this chapter is one of the most detailed ones in *A Declaration*.

Arminius did not skirt the issue of predestination, nor did he avoid the controversial topics tossed at him earlier by Gomarus in

---

6. Arminius, *A Declaration of Sentiments*, 29.
7. Wood, "The Declaration of Sentiments," 115.
8. Arminius, *A Declaration of Sentiments*, 56.

their debates. Instead, he confidently and carefully presented his views on predestination, first elaborating his Supralapsarian opponents' arguments which are "... both false and impertinent, and at an utter disagreement with each other."[9] Then, when he has finished critically challenging their Supralapsarian suppositions, Arminius presented his own views, calling on Scripture, the Confession, and logic for support.

He finished his argument by stating, "It is therefore much to be desired, that men would proceed no further in this matter, and would not attempt to investigate the unsearchable judgments of God—at least that they would not proceed beyond the point at which those judgments have been clearly revealed in the scriptures."[10] He perceived the misjudgments of his opponents to be an extreme distortion of interpretation, manifested by their making doctrinal decisions not explicitly found or supported in Scripture. Arminius went on to link the matter of predestination with other theological aspects; however, he does not go into the same amount of detail and examination with each chapter.

Most parts of *A Declaration* are brief, although Arminius does devote extra material to a few sections (I, VII, VIII, X), which will be discussed in the next chapter. Section II considers the providence of God. Section III examines the Free-Will of Man. Section IV describes the grace of God. Section V discusses the perseverance of the saints. Section VI deals with the assurance of salvation. Section VII focuses on the perfection of the believer. Section VIII investigates the divinity of Christ at some length. Section IX looks at the justification of the believer. In section X, Arminius offers his own revision to the Dutch Confession and the Heidelberg Catechism along with some cautious advice.

Arminius concluded his *Declaration of Sentiments* with an acknowledgement of submission to the assembly's authority and power. Twice calling them his "most noble, potent, wise and prudent masters,"[11] he thanked them for their patience and courtesy

---

9. Ibid., 69.
10. Ibid., 166–167.
11. Ibid., 3 and 232.

during his presentation and assured them that he wanted nothing less than to heal the conflict between himself and his attackers.

Showing what could be considered humility and diplomacy, Arminius claimed, "I also make this additional promise, that I will in every conference conduct myself with equanimity, moderation and docility, and will shew myself not less actuated by the desire of being taught, than by that of communicating to others some portion of instruction."[12] The heart of this statement is his reiteration that his goals have always been the reconciliation with his brothers (and sisters, no doubt) in Christ and the promotion of healthy understanding of the plan of God.

A Declaration of Sentiments was created during a pivotal time in Arminius' life. For years, his attackers had been attempting to humiliate him in the religious sphere. Unhappily for them, Arminius presented his case with an "eloquence and moderation"[13] that frustrated their attempts at crushing his biblical and doctrinal interpretations. He may not have succeeded in convincing them of the error of their ways, but neither did they stamp out a theology that they considered so dangerously heretical.

The heated analysis of Arminius' theological writings continued after his death and presently is still a matter of debate. Both Calvinist and Arminian have sought to demonstrate either the error or success of Arminius' theological approach in his writings. On account of this, numerous theologians and scholars have scrutinized *A Declaration* and its author. However, before attempting to ascertain the state of scholarly judgment on *A Declaration of Sentiments*, an analysis of its textual content will be pursued in the next chapter.

---

12. Ibid., 233.

13. Harrison, *The Beginnings of Arminianism*, 111.

5

Detailed Analysis of a Declaration of Sentiments

THIS INVESTIGATION NOW MOVES from the previous general overview to a deeper examination of *A Declaration of Sentiments*. In the years preceding the creation of his *Declaration*, Arminius frequently defended his position as a minister and theologian in the Reformed church and as a supporter of Calvin. *A Declaration* is the summary compilation of that defensive effort against the Supralapsarians and high Calvinists. As such, each section of *A Declaration* will be inspected as to its topic(s), thesis statement, and supportive assertions.

A Declaration consists of ten chapters on a variety of topics, but Arminius did not dwell equally in consideration on each of them. With clear purpose in mind, he gave appropriate attention to the aspects of doctrine crucial for a better awareness of his position, and in order to obtain a fuller understanding of the relationship between humanity and God. As such, he hoped his presentation would serve a dual purpose in his endeavors for biblical truth and in his defense of Supralapsarian charges.

Section I—"On Predestination"

This is by far the most complex part of *A Declaration*. Nearly 15,000 words long, this exposition has three purposes. First, Arminius describes the Supralapsarian understanding of predestination and explains how it is harmful and wrong. Second, he presents other views of predestination with their finer points of understanding and benefit. Last, Arminius presents his own views on predestination.

Arminius' depiction of the Supralapsarian understanding regarding this topic is unflattering, to say the least. He began his examination with a blunt statement of dismissal of their assertion that God has predestined some to salvation and others to damnation. He points out the fact that it is a belief ". . . espoused by those [Supralapsarians] who assume the very highest ground of this Predestination."[1] So began his condemnation of their extremist doctrinal interpretation of Calvin and the Bible.

He then went on to detail their arguments and later provided the grounds for his rejection of these theological opinions. The main reasons for his denunciation of the Supralapsarian position included the following: (1) "It is not the foundation of Christianity, of Salvation, or of its certainty,"[2] (2) it ". . . comprises within it neither the whole nor any part of the Gospel,"[3] and (3) it ". . . was never admitted, decreed, or approved in any Council, either general or particular, for the first six hundred years after Christ."[4]

Supplementing this, he added, it ". . . neither agrees nor corresponds with the Harmony of those Confessions which were printed and published together in one Volume at Geneva, in the name of the Reformed and Protestant Churches,"[5] it is ". . . repugnant to the Nature of God,"[6] it is ". . . opposed to the Act of

---

1. Arminius, *A Declaration of Sentiments*, 58.
2. Ibid., 73.
3. Ibid., 75.
4. Ibid., 78.
5. Ibid., 81.
6. Ibid., 88.

Creation,"[7] it is ". . . injurious to the Glory of God,"[8] it is ". . . hurtful to the salvation of men,"[9] and it ". . . is in open hostility to the Ministry of the Gospel."[10]

Apparently, Arminius had little trouble pointing out the defects of the Supralapsarian approach to predestination. He backed up each of these criticisms with proof of their flawed foundations. This long list is a testament to his personal disdain for the doctrine promoted by these high Calvinists.

Arminius then went on to describe two other incorrect ways of conceptualizing predestination other than that of the Supralapsarians. First, God irreversibly decided in eternity,

> . . . to make (according to his own good pleasure) the smaller portion out of the general mass of mankind partakers of his grace and glory, to the praise of his own glorious grace. But according to his pleasure he also passed by the greater portion of men, and left them in their own nature, which is incapable of every thing supernatural [or beyond itself], and did not communicate to them that saving and supernatural grace by which their nature (if it still retained its integrity), might be strengthened, or by which, if it were corrupted, it might be restored—for a demonstration of his own liberty. Yet, after God had made these men sinners and guilty of death, he punished them with death eternal—for a demonstration of his own justice.[11]

The crux of this complex passage is the suggestion that Arminius finds no logic or love in God predestining some people to salvation and others to damnation. Whether it is before or after the Fall of Adam—both seem incongruous considering God's expressed plan in Scripture for humanity.

Arminius rejected this understanding because it makes God the author of sin, which he cannot and will not affirm. Furthermore,

7. Ibid., 96.
8. Ibid., 105.
9. Ibid., 110.
10. Ibid., 116.
11. Ibid., 140.

this concept suggests an understanding of predestination that is "... a palpable and absurd self-contradiction."[12] It does not fit into any logical understanding of the nature of humanity nor does it accommodate God's biblical plan of redemption.

Arminius described another understanding of predestination in which "God acts without the least consideration of repentance and faith in those whom he elects, or of impenitence and unbelief in those whom he reprobates."[13] Arminius condemned this third understanding of predestination because it suggests that God does not care about the moral behavior or authentic faith of His followers—a concept not found in Scripture. This concept conflicts with the image of the God of justice accepted by early church fathers. God carefully judges the world and all its inhabitants, suggesting that He would not arbitrarily send certain people to heaven and hell, regardless of their good or bad faith in Him.

Finally, Arminius presented his own understanding of predestination. Rather than the lengthy exercise used earlier to invalidate the Supralapsarian view, Arminius offered a short and concise argument for his beliefs in this matter. He pointed to four decrees of God as evidence for his standpoint.

First, God "... decreed to appoint his Son, Jesus Christ, for a Mediator, Redeemer, saviour, Priest and King, who might destroy sin by his own death, might by his obedience obtain the salvation which had been lost, and might communicate it by his own virtue."[14] Jesus Christ is the ultimate sin offering used to appropriate the complete salvation of all humanity. Second, God "... decreed to receive into favour those who repent and believe, and, in Christ, for his sake and through Him, to effect the salvation of such penitents and Believers as persevered to the end."[15] Remaining in a sinful state only leads to death and to eternal damnation, but turning from sin leads to personal salvation. Third, "God decreed to administer in a sufficient and efficacious manner the means which

12. Ibid., 152.
13. Ibid., 146.
14. Ibid., 158.
15. Ibid.

were necessary for repentance and faith."[16] The resources for finding one's salvation are always available to everyone because God is ultimately wise, merciful, and just. Fourth,

> He knew from all eternity those individuals who would, through his preventing grace, believe, and, through his subsequent grace would persevere, according to the before described administration of those means which are suitable and proper for conversion and faith; and, by which foreknowledge, he likewise knew those who would not believe and persevere.[17]

This is not the same as ordaining some to salvation and others to perdition; rather, it is a supernatural ability to see into all possibilities of humanity and the future. It speaks of the power of God, which, conveniently, Arminius discusses in the next section in his *Declaration*.

Section II—"The Providence of God"

This section focuses on the providence or guardianship of God in regards to the world and its inhabitants. Defending himself against accusations of Pelagianism, he used inclusive language to describe the sovereignty and power of God. He wanted no one to misunderstand his intentions or beliefs in this matter. For Arminius, God is supremely in charge.

Even though it is presented as one long paragraph—in essence, this section is comprised of three sub-sections. The first dwells on the overall providence of God, the second states God's role in acts of goodness and evil, and the third section is a refutation of allegations against him. Ultimately, his goal was to allow his audience greater insight into his beliefs on God's divine intervention in life, thereby acquitting himself of Supralapsarian accusations.

Arminius began this section with a blanket statement describing the providence of God:

16. Ibid., 159.
17. Ibid., 159–160.

> I consider Divine Providence to be that solicitous, continued, and universally present inspection and oversight of God, according to which he exercises a general care over the whole world, but evinces a particular concern for all his [intelligent] creatures without any exception, with the design of preserving and governing them in their own essence, qualities, actions, and passions, in a manner that is at once worthy of himself and suitable to them, to the praise of his name and the salvation of Believers.[18]

As one can see from this verbose sentence, Arminius' beliefs on the providence of God are multidimensional. However, some key words and ideas stand out. First, "Providence" concerns the oversight of God. He is transcendent and omnipotent in His divine duties. Second, God is lovingly active in the world according to His nature and despite humanity's nature. Third, attesting to God's ultimate dominion in life, ". . . nothing in the world happens fortuitously or by chance."[19] The governance of God includes the actions and free-will of every individual.

The next sub-section deals with the origin of good and evil. Arminius states, "God both wills and performs good acts but that He only freely permits those which are evil."[20] Thus, God is the author of good, but not of evil. Arminius wanted his listeners not to misunderstand him on this aspect.

The third section points to allegations "falsely imputed"[21] against him and challenges their validity based on the statements in this chapter as well as other documents. Arminius concluded this section with his own allegation of serious misconduct on the part of his attackers.

---

18. Ibid., 169.
19. Ibid., 170.
20. Ibid.
21. Ibid., 172.

Section III—"The Free-Will of Man"

This section is the shortest in *A Declaration*, but it is not without some significance. In it, Arminius described the reality of humanity's exercise of free-will on earth. In an attempt to dispel more rumors of Pelagianism, as with the previous section, Arminius used appropriate language to convey the hegemony of God. Despite God's dominion, though, humanity has been endowed with some abilities to choose autonomously; however, human will only exists in conjunction with the grace of God.

> In his primitive condition as he came out of the hands of his creator, man was endowed with such a portion of knowledge, holiness and power, as enabled him to understand, esteem, consider, will, and to perform the true good, according to the commandment delivered to him. Yet, none of these acts could he do, except through the assistance of Divine Grace.[22]

Thus, God creates the will of a human being, but it can only be used with God's help. Arminius supports this notion when he remarks, ". . . man is not capable, of and by himself, either to think, to will, or to do that which is really good."[23] Humanity is still utterly dependent upon God despite possessing some volitional autonomy.

Another aspect of this section that needs attention is Arminius' belief in the "synergistic" relationship of God and humanity. Much to the annoyance of his Supralapsarian opponents, Arminius used incendiary phrases like, "Man was endowed,"[24] "through the assistance,"[25] and "made a partaker."[26] These statements suggest a joint endeavor that incorporates the actions of humanity with God's will—a definite high Calvinist faux pas considering their monergistic[27] position.

22. Ibid., 173.
23. Ibid.
24. Ibid.
25. Ibid.
26. Ibid., 174.
27. According to Kirkpatrick, "Monergism is the belief that the work of

Assuredly, most extreme Calvinists would consider this understanding unorthodox and contrary to proper doctrine. However, Arminius does not defend his position at all, which seems peculiar as he is often considered to be pro-Catholic in this understanding.[28] This may be where Arminius departs from complete Calvinist adherence, however.[29] Perhaps he did not elaborate fully fearing his explanations would only provide his enemies with more "ammunition" to use against him.

Section IV—"The Grace of God"

This next section examines God's grace, its nature and effect on humanity, and its existence in an individual's life. It is comprised of three sub-sections. The first two are descriptive; the last is a brief defense of Arminius' unique perspective on grace.

The first sub-section details the nature and description of divine grace. The grace of God is crucial in the presentation of *A Declaration*. In many ways, it is the "glue" that holds Arminius' defense together against the attacks of the high Calvinists.

He breaks down grace to three points. First, grace is unwarranted, "gratuitous affection"[30] from God to the sinner, providing eternal life, justification, and adoption. Grace is also an ". . . infusion . . . of all those gifts of the Holy Spirit which appertain to the regeneration and renewing of man."[31] These gifts only come from God; without them, humanity can do no good act. Finally, grace is ". . . that perpetual assistance and continued aid of the Holy Spirit"[32] that inspires humanity to act in good ways for the glory of God.

The next sub-section in this chapter focuses on the influence of grace on human behavior. It is the catalyst for all good and

---

salvation is by God alone." Kirpatrick, *Monergism or Synergism*, xi.
28. Olson, *The Story of Christian Theology*, 461.
29. See chapter six for details.
30. Arminius, *A Declaration of Sentiments*, 175.
31. Ibid., 175–176.
32. Ibid., 176.

loving actions. If an individual is behaving in godly fashion, it is solely due to the presence of God's grace asserting its influence. In consideration of this, Arminius asserted, "A man, though already regenerate, can neither conceive, will, nor do any good at all, nor resist any evil temptation, without this preventing and exciting, this following and co-operating grace."[33]

True, Arminius believed in the free-will of man to do beneficial deeds; however, this ability is only in existence through the grace of God alone.[34] There is no other source for it—an understanding deflating Supralapsarian claims of Arminius being a Pelagian or Socinian.

The last sub-section deals with the matter of resisting the Holy Spirit. Whereas his Supralapsarian adversaries contend that no human being can resist the Spirit of God, Arminius pointed to scripture and stated, "I believe, according to the scriptures, that many persons resist the Holy Spirit and reject the grace that is offered."[35] He did not dispute what can be accomplished with the help of the grace of God; he only suggested that it is not beyond rejection. He pointed out that though the nature of grace is observable both in life and in the Bible, its mode is more mysterious. This matter would be dealt with more definitively in Holland at the Synod of Dort in 1618.

Section V—"The Perseverance of the Saints"

This section is very intriguing for it deals with the matter of the perseverance of the saints—that is, the continued victory over sin in the life of the believer and an uninterrupted relationship with God. The first sub-section deals with what perseverance is and how it is maintained. The second sub-section, though, brings up a question over the possibility of a believer falling away from the faith. Arminius addressed the doctrine of perseverance.

33. Ibid.
34. A factor often espoused by John Wesley in his book, *A Plain Account of Christian Perfection* (Schmul, 1988).
35. Arminius, *A Declaration of Sentiments*, 177.

> My sentiments respecting the perseverance of the saints are, that those persons who have been grafted into Christ by true faith, and have thus been made partakers of his life-giving Spirit, possess sufficient powers [or strength] to fight against Satan, sin, the world and their own flesh, and to gain the victory over these enemies—yet not without the assistance of the grace of the same Holy Spirit.[36]

He suggested that every Christian has the resources, provided by God, to resist the powers of evil in order to maintain a healthy relationship with God. There is no danger of being ". . . either seduced or dragged out of the hands of Christ,"[37] or of being impotent in one's earnest attempt to keep the faith. God provides his grace and its benefits in order to enable each believer to succeed.

This appears to fall in line with proper Reformed thought; however, the second sub-section questions whether willful disobedience and rejection can ". . . cause Divine grace to be ineffectual."[38] Thus, Arminius contended that it is impossible to have one's position with God taken away, although it may be possible to turn away from it. Always using Scripture as the foundation, Arminius noted "certain passages"[39] that seem to suggest the latter. This approach flies in the face of the eternal determinism of the Supralapsarians.

Section VI—"The Assurance of Salvation"

As with the perseverance of the saints, Arminius suggested that it is possible to have good confidence that one's salvation is not so fragile as to require perpetual anxiety and fear. However, Arminius reminded the reader that no human is the eternal judge—God is. Therefore, there is some room for speculation and contemplation on the part of the believer.

This chapter consists of two sub-sections. The first details Arminius' opinion of what assurance of salvation means. He states,

36. Ibid., 178.
37. Ibid., 179.
38. Ibid.
39. Ibid., 180.

Detailed Analysis of a Declaration of Sentiments

"It is possible for him who believes in Jesus Christ to be certain and persuaded, and, if his heart condemn him not, he is now in reality assured, that he is a son of God, and stands in the grace of Jesus Christ."[40] This belief should be both heart-felt and intellectually perceived. Moreover, this belief is actualized by ". . . the testimony of God's Spirit witnessing together with his conscience."[41] Still, one should not forget that God is the ultimate judge and that every believer is still reliant upon God for his or her salvation.

In the second sub-section, Arminius subtly raises an issue regarding any absolute certitude on soteriology as an item for debate. He does not state his opinion one way or another but remarks, "Yet, it will be proper to make the extent of the boundaries of this assurance, a subject of inquiry in our convention."[42] Without a great deal of Scriptural proof or early church father definitive explanations, Arminius saw aspects of this doctrine open to debate and discussion. The double predestination of Calvinism makes this assurance seem absolute—a quality that Arminius would suggest is more speculative that definitive, and an approach that steps dangerously close to the prohibited act of eternal judgment by mortal beings with limited perspectives.

Section VII—"The Perfection of Believers in This Life"

In this chapter, Arminius brings up the fact that he has been accused of Pelagianism because of his speculation that a believer can live a sinless life. "It is reported, that I entertain sentiments on this subject, which are very improper, and nearly allied to those of the Pelagians."[43] However, the error of his attackers is that they fail to acknowledge the caveat he includes in his understanding of perfection. With his understanding that nothing happens without the direction of God, Arminius states, "It

40. Ibid., 181.
41. Ibid., 182.
42. Ibid.
43. Ibid., 184.

is possible for the regenerate in this life perfectly to keep God's precepts."⁴⁴ He then went on to show how he was only promoting ideas similar to those of St. Augustine.⁴⁵

He continued, "Though these might have been my sentiments, yet I ought not on this account to be considered a Pelagian, either partly or entirely, provided I had only added that 'they could do this by the grace of Christ, and by no means without it.'"⁴⁶ As with earlier chapters, Arminius made sure to keep the grace of God as the crucial element in his doctrine. Arminius defended himself by remarking that he never asserted that a person can live free from sin, but he never denied it, either (adding to suspicions of Arminius being a Pelagian).

He appealed to the great church father, Augustine, whose own statements suggested the possibility of perfection. Furthermore, he pointed to the absurdity of his opponents accusing him of being a Pelagian when his ideas merely mirror those of Augustine, ". . . one of the most strenuous adversaries of the Pelagian doctrine."⁴⁷ Beyond this, Arminius proclaimed, "I account this sentiment of Pelagius to be heretical, and diametrically opposed to these words of Christ, 'Without me ye can do nothing' (John xv, 5.)"⁴⁸ Arminius wanted no misunderstanding of his condemnation of Pelagius and his own promotion of the authority of Scripture.

Arminius ended this chapter lamenting the misrepresentation of him by his critics. He assured his audience that what information is being spread about him by men like Gomarus is based only on rumor. He then informs his listeners/readers that he is going to ". . . disclose to your mightinesses the real state of the whole matter,"⁴⁹ which he does in the next chapter.

---

44. Ibid.

45. St. Augustine is considered by some to be the greatest theologian of the early Church. His interpretations of biblical truth began the usage of the terms orthodoxy and heresy.

46. Arminius, *A Declaration of Sentiments*, 184–185.

47. Ibid, 187.

48. Ibid., 188.

49. Ibid., 189–190.

Section VIII—"The Divinity of the Son of God"

Section VIII, as with Section I, is one of the most difficult passages to examine because of its sophisticated theological arguments. In it, Arminius sought to defend himself against attacks that he is spreading unorthodox views about the deity of Christ. In this chapter, he also attempted to prove that his detractors are using an unfair standard against him.

According to Arminius, the whole matter revolves around the interpretation of the word, αυτοθεόν—a Greek word meaning "very God," "one who is truly God," or "one who is of God of himself."[50] Arminius claimed this word was used incorrectly by many of his fellow professors at Leyden and that it carries with it the possibility of ". . . two mutually conflicting errors"[51]—Tritheism and Sabellianism.[52] Furthermore, his criticism of its usage is based on both Scripture, the works of the Church Fathers, and orthodox doctrine established long before his time.

Regarding the confusing nature of the term, he asserted, "Yet the proceeding of the origin of one person from another (that is, of the Son from the Father), is the only foundation that has ever been used for defending the Unity of the Divine Essence in the Trinity of Persons."[53]

According to Arminius, αυτοθεόν denotes something else than that. He added,

> For, these two things, to be the Son and to be God, are at perfect agreement with each other; but to derive his essence from the Father, and, at the same time, to derive it from no one, are evidently contradictory, and mutually destructive the one of the other.[54]

---

50. Ibid.
51. Ibid., 194.
52. Tritheism is the heretical teaching about the Trinity that denies the unity of substance in the Divine Persons. Sabellianism is an alternative name for the Modalist form of Monarchianism.
53. Arminius, *A Declaration of Sentiments*, 194.
54. Ibid., 200.

The term suggests equality to the point that the different personages are either blurred or harshly separated—a concept condemned by him and even his opponents, when it suits their agenda. Arminius unveiled this prejudiced approach of his critics when he comments,

> No one endeavoured to vindicate me from this calumny; while great exertion was employed to frame excuses for Trelcatius, by means of a qualified interpretation of his words, though it was utterly impossible to reconcile their palliative explanations with the plain signification of his unperverted expressions. Such are the effects which the partiality of favour and the fervour of zeal can produce![55]

The remainder of the chapter is devoted to dissecting the understanding of the essence of God and Christ more thoroughly. His goal is the transmission of his clear, traditional, orthodox understanding of the Trinity. He has been accused of limiting the divinity of Christ because he does not like the term, αυτοθεόν. For Arminius, however, the term itself is unorthodox and unscriptural. As such, he stated, "Therefore, in no way whatever can this phrase . . . be excused as a correct one, or as having been happily expressed."[56]

As with other doctrinal matters, if it is not in Scripture, it can only be considered conjecturally. Arminius finished the section with a "kidney punch" of his own, insinuating that his opponents were truly hypocritical in their theological positions. In their use of αυτοθεόν, they were the ones spreading dangerous extra-Trinitarian doctrine.

Section IX—"The Justification of Man Before God"

Arminius' chapter on justification serves two purposes. First, it demonstrates how affable Arminius was in this controversy.

---

55. Ibid., 197.
56. Ibid., 202.

Detailed Analysis of a Declaration of Sentiments

Second, it reinforces Arminius' keeping with Calvinist thought. Concerning the first point, Arminius discussed an on-going debate between the French churches and various professors of theology.

> I never durst mingle myself with the dispute, or undertake to decide it; for I thought it possible for the Professors of the same religion to hold different opinions on this point from others of their brethren, without any breach of Christian peace or the unity of faith. Similar peaceful thoughts appear to have been indulged by both the adverse parties in this dispute; for they exercised a friendly toleration towards each other, and did not make that a reason for mutually renouncing their fraternal concord.[57]

Arminius saw this debate as an opportunity for theologians to graciously demonstrate their Christian charity in the midst of controversy—unlike his own experience with the Supralapsarians who he concludes are hostile gentlemen "of a different judgment."[58] His subtle comparison effectively described his version of the unloving and unwarranted attacks of his opponents. Arminius' words on Reformed thought (and especially on John Calvin) make this mistreatment appear even more inappropriate.

He began this chapter with a statement of agreement. He declared, "I am not conscious to myself, of having taught or entertained any other sentiments concerning the justification of man before God than those which are held unanimously by the Reformed and Protestant Churches, and which are in complete agreement with their expressed opinions.[59] Unlike some other issues of doctrine, Arminius saw little to disagree with in his opponents' approach to this topic. Complementing this is Arminius' proclamation concerning Calvin.

> Yet, my opinion is not so widely different from his as to prevent me from employing the signature of my own hand in subscribing to those things which he has delivered on this subject, in the third book of his Institutes;

---

57. Ibid., 205–206.
58. Ibid., 206.
59. Ibid., 204.

this I am prepared to do at any time, and to give them my full approval."[60]

His opponents accused him of being an enemy of the Reformed faith and of Calvinism. Arminius' assertions completely rejected this notion and with these words, Arminius ended the formal part of his *Declaration of Sentiments*. He provided the Assembly that which they have requested—a statement of doctrine on various issues. He stated, "Most noble and potent Lords, these are the principal articles, respecting which I have judged it necessary to declare my opinion before this august meeting, in obedience to your commands."[61] However, he also imparted perhaps more than they expected. He provided substantiating proof for both his Reformed views and a defense against the Supralapsarian. His *Declaration* was nearly over, except for one more contribution to the agenda of the Assembly.

Section X—"The Revision of the Dutch Confession and the Heidelberg Catechism"

The last chapter of Arminius' *Declaration of Sentiments* focused on the possibility of the calling of a national Synod in Holland. Basically, this section elaborates on three desires of Arminius. First, it is an endorsement for a national Synod for a variety of reasons to be explained shortly. Second, it is an appeal for proper conduct to be maintained in the activities of the Synod. Third, it calls for proper and reasonable discussion, debate, and doctrinal investigation. Fourth, it pleads for Confessional simplicity and clarity.

Contrary to what his opponents may have thought, Arminius was more than eager for a national Synod to be called. He stated, "It is obviously agreeable to reason as well as to equity, and quite necessary in the present posture of affairs, that such a measure should be adopted."[62] Arminius did not fear the idea of a holistic examination

---

60. Ibid., 209.
61. Ibid.
62. Ibid., 212.

Detailed Analysis of a Declaration of Sentiments

of the doctrinal confession of the Dutch Church—it could help to ease the hostile environment he observed around him. Furthermore, a Synod could control Supralapsarian thought containing "far too many particulars."[63] It also could legitimize the idea that parts of the Bible are mysterious and above dogmatic thought. It could additionally promote an approach to theology that is not as myopic and rigid regarding doctrinal priorities. Thus, Arminius embraced the idea of future scrutiny over the Confession.

Arminius further advised the Assembly to run the Synod, reasonably and fairly.

> If the Church be properly instructed in that difference which really does and always ought to exist between the word of God and all human writings, and if the Church be also rightly informed concerning that liberty which she and all Christians possess, and which they will always enjoy, to measure all human compositions by the standard rule of God's word, she will neither distress herself on that account, nor will she be offended on perceiving all human writings brought to be proved at the touch-stone of God's word.[64]

This is the summation of what Arminius considered wrong with the current state of religious affairs in Holland. The inflexibility and fear of his opponents had so tainted the process that true doctrinal analysis is being stalled and hampered. The Reformed Church had to be able to examine its doctrine—else contamination and calamity could sneak into the Confession. Despite this, Arminius graciously acknowledged the validity of some parts of his opponents' opinion.

> Some points in the Confession are certain and do not admit of a doubt: these will never be called in question by any one, except by heretics. Yet, there are other parts of its contents which are of such a kind, as may with the most obvious utility become frequent subjects of conference and discussion between men of learning who fear

63. Ibid., 214.
64. Ibid., 225.

God, for the purpose of reconciling them with those indubitable articles as nearly as is practicable.[65]

Arminius attempted to bridge the differences and to reach his opponents. He was an advocate for his understanding of Scripture and doctrine, but he was not trying to be tyrannical about it. In his concluding address, Arminius testified, "For I am not of the congregation of those who wish to have dominion over the faith of another man, but am only a minister to Believers, with the design of promoting in them an increase of knowledge, truth, piety, peace and joy in Jesus Christ our Lord."[66] Arminius created *A Declaration of Sentiments* with this in mind.

Using Scripture, Reformed thought, the Confession, his opponents' words (as well as his own), Arminius sought to successfully weave a defense of his theology and actions. Examining each section carefully, one could see the difficult task he had in defending himself against the Supralapsarians. He not only had to prove that he was innocent of their charges; he also had to demonstrate the weaknesses of their arguments. Like near-sighted sailors attempting to chart the stars, he felt their descriptions of God's plan were blurry and misleading. *A Declaration* was his attempt to bring the doctrinal truths expressed in the Bible into better focus, for healing and reconciliation between the battling camps.

Whether he was successful or not greatly depends upon one's theological position, of course. In the next chapter, various scholars speak to Arminius' efforts in *A Declaration* and provide their judgments of his defense against the Supralapsarians.

---

65. Ibid., 229–230.
66. Ibid., 235.

6

Scholarly Voices on a Declaration of Sentiments

THIS CHAPTER WILL TAKE a closer look at assorted scholarly opinions about Arminius and his *Declaration of Sentiments*. By examining the opinions of multiple scholars from various camps of theological thought concerning the issues addressed in *A Declaration*, hopefully a more complete understanding of Arminius' theology and thought can be perceived, especially in how it pertains to his conflict with the high Calvinists.

For purposes of this chapter, four general concerns regarding Arminius and *A Declaration of Sentiments* are examined. The first matter will briefly focus on the general presentation of *A Declaration*; the second will examine Arminius' response concerning the controversial question of predestination; the third will examine Arminius' relationship with the Reformed thought of Calvin; and the last will detail Arminius' ultimate goals for his *Declaration*, specifically that of reconciliation and unity.

The Presentation of A Declaration

As detailed in chapter five, Arminius wrote *A Declaration of Sentiments* in response to the accusations of the Supralapsarian party

55

that he was promoting theology in disagreement with Reformed thought. In *A Declaration*, Arminius sought not only to prove that he was in line with Calvinism, but also that his opponents were in error in their own understanding of several important tenets of Christianity. At the outset, Arminius hoped to completely dispel the rumors and misunderstandings about him and his theology by succinctly presenting his case.

Many scholars feel he managed well in this endeavor. Wood remarks, "The clear and unequivocal *Declaration of Sentiments* represents the mature conclusions of the reformer in response to those who doubted whether his interpretations were compatible with the doctrinal standards of the Dutch Church."[1] Carl Bangs similarly states, "He spoke firmly and openly, attacking what he found in the church that he felt was wrong, and offering a clear exposition of his own views at those points which were controverted."[2] Gunter concludes, "The assembly of the States General in The Hague was satisfied. The theologian's views were comfortably within the parameters of acceptable Reformed theology. Within a year, tuberculosis claimed his life, and he died in the good graces of his beloved Reformed Church."[3]

Each of these scholars affirm Arminius' dual purposes for *A Declaration* and credit him for its clarity and persuasiveness.

Predestination and A Declaration

Beyond its well-communicated delivery, *A Declaration* focuses on some important doctrinal controversies in the relationship between Arminius and the high Calvinists. Among others, this includes Pelagianism, Arianism, and Socinianism. First and foremost, however, *A Declaration of Sentiments* responds to the attacks of the Supralapsarians against Arminius' approach to predestination.

---

1. Wood, "The Declaration of Sentiments," 111–112.
2. Bangs, *Arminius*, 308.
3. Gunter, *Arminius and His Declaration of Sentiments*, 191.

As addressed earlier, Arminius felt the Supralapsarians had taken too rigid a position on this mysterious aspect of God not explicitly defined in Scripture. Thus, he openly disagreed with their doctrinal interpretation and went to some effort to disprove it in *A Declaration*. Bangs writes, "His [Arminius] most terse, systematic, and mature statement of his position is that of the *Declaration of Sentiments*, where he defines the doctrine [of predestination]."[4] In this definition, Arminius points to four parameters ignored by his opponents: Christology, evangelicalism, responsibility, and orthodoxy.

According to Bangs, Arminius has defended his position well that he has always kept with Reformed thought and the Dutch Church. Yet, this scholar further suggests that Arminius, "... gives his case away"[5] in his deliberations with Gomarus with his promotion of the activities of God as being both a relationship and a historical concern. This dualism seems contradictory to the modern mind. Overall, though, Bangs claims that Arminius "... had a high degree of success in meeting the criteria which he had established for an evangelical doctrine of predestination."[6] Cameron adds his scholarly voice to the discussion when he states that Arminius understands predestination "... in terms of this interpretation of the relationship between foreknowledge and predestination."[7]

For the Calvinist, predestination concerns God's providential guiding, whereas Arminius would argue it concerns God's supernatural knowledge of what will happen in the future. Furthermore, Arminius appears to be advocating an understanding of salvation for both the individual and a general class of believers. As reported by Cameron, this leads Arminius into "difficulties"[8] and leaves him "open to criticism"[9] because of his seeming self-contradiction. As Peterson and Williams assert, "An Arminian is

4. Bangs, *Arminius*, 350.
5. Ibid., 353.
6. Ibid., 354.
7. Cameron, "Arminius—Hero or Heretic?" 220.
8. Ibid.
9. Ibid.

by definition not a Calvinist, and a Calvinist could not also be an Arminian."[10]

Lutzer also expounds on the election of the believer. According to Lutzer, Arminius professed that all people are called to join God's kingdom. The Dutch Reformer was ". . . persuaded of the doctrine of free will and universal grace."[11] Countering this, Calvinist doctrine states that some are elected to salvation; others are elected to perdition. Lutzer suggests that the problem of Arminius' approach is that it ". . . denies the two truths the Scripture proclaims, namely, that God did the choosing and that the choice was made prior to creation."[12]

Wood clarifies the issue even more in his approving analysis of *A Declaration of Sentiments*. Concerning predestination, Wood states, "We may therefore assume that his treatment in the *Declaration* reflects his considered judgment"[13] Pointing to at least twenty reasons why Supralapsarian predestination is incorrect, Arminius uses not only logic, but also biblical support to defend his position. Wood notes that unlike earlier "restrained"[14] writings, Arminius' criticisms of the Supralapsarians in *A Declaration* are "sufficiently trenchant."[15] Arminius' approach in his *Declaration* is not especially gentle, but rather is sharply fixed. Wood ends his article with great praise. "It also enshrines the quintessence of Arminius' teaching on a series of vital and yet often debatable topics."[16]

Although each of these scholars offers differing degrees of approval concerning Arminius and *A Declaration*, none suggest that he explicitly has failed in his effort to defend his theological position on predestination. *A Declaration*, however, was not limited to the doctrinal matter of predestination alone. In later sections of

---

10. Peterson and Williams, *Why I Am Not an Arminian*, 9.
11. Lutzer, *The Doctrines That Divide*, 178.
12. Ibid., 182.
13. Wood, "The Declaration of Sentiments," 116.
14. Ibid., 119.
15. Ibid.
16. Ibid., 129.

his treatise, Arminius goes on to defend himself against further accusations of the high Calvinists.

Calvinism and A Declaration

Arminius' Agreement with Calvinism

Reading through *A Declaration*, it is evident that Arminius' theology does not explicitly contradict Reformed, Calvinist theology as much as frequently reported in some circles. It is true that Arminius does promote specific changes in interpreting doctrinal conclusions, but on the whole, he remains mostly within the boundaries of Reformed thought.

In his article, "Arminius and the Scholastic Tradition," Muller writes, "Although there was little love lost between Arminius and his Reformed Predestinarian colleagues at Leiden, he shared with them a genuine affinity for 'Calvinist Thomism' of major Reformed teachers of the preceding generations."[17] Not only is Arminius defending himself, but he also is perpetually seeking to show connections between his theological understandings and the Reformed Church's views.

In agreement with this concept, Bangs writes, "It may be concluded that on the doctrine of the church, Arminius stood within the broad Reformed tradition."[18] H

---

17. Muller, "Arminius and the Scholastic Tradition," 275.
18. Bangs, *Arminius*, 337.

He further includes, "It should be apparent by now that Arminius worked within both the ecclesiastical and intellectual structure of the Reformed Church."[19] It is Bangs' contention that Arminius was not acting against the Reformed Church as a heretic or enemy; rather, Arminius was merely striving to clarify controversial issues for the Reformational benefit of the whole Church body (which happened to include himself).

Sell further substantiates Arminius' agreement with mainstream Calvinism and the Catechism, "Arminius had no difficulty with the Heidelberg Catechism . . . This was a legitimate and legally correct interpretation before the Synod of Dort."[20] Sell suggests that Arminius' theological approach demonstrates unity with all the Reformed and Protestant churches[21] at that time. His disagreements were only with the extreme Supralapsarian interpretation of doctrine.

Even though ultimately he proclaims pivotal differences between the accepted doctrines of Arminius and Calvin, R. C. Sproul admits, "Arminius himself came from a Calvinistic framework and embraced many tenets of historic Calvinism"[22] and that Arminius ". . . held Calvin and his work in high regard."[23] As suggested by Sproul and other scholars, Arminius apparently was not completely at war with High Calvinism; however, clear differences can be observed between Arminius' doctrine and strict Calvinist thought.

Arminius' Departure From Calvinism

Despite these scholarly testimonies of Arminius' agreement with Reformed thought, Arminius unmistakably departs from Calvinistic doctrine in some crucial ways. The TULIP doctrine (Total Depravity, Unconditional Election, Limited Atonement, Irresistibility

---

19. Bangs, *Arminius*, 333.
20. Sell, *The Great Debate*, 12.
21. Ibid., 12.
22. Sproul, *Willing to Believe*, 126.
23. Ibid.

of Grace, Perseverance of the Saints) created after Arminius' death dramatically demonstrates the difference of thought between Arminius and Supralapsarianism. As Rice puts it, "The concept of absolute foreknowledge retained from Calvinism is incompatible with the dynamic portrait of God that is basic to Arminianism."[24]

As mentioned previously, Arminius felt that the mystery of God excluded the absolute doctrinal position that the Supralapsarians were suggesting. To him, the topic of divine election required more study to be made before concluding. Yet, in some ways, this position appears to contradict mainstream Calvinist thought.

In the *Institutes* (1536), Calvin states, "We call predestination God's eternal decree, by which he compacted with himself what he willed to become of each man. For all are not created in equal condition; rather, eternal life is foreordained for some, eternal damnation for others."[25] Statements such as these from Calvin appear to hurt Arminius' case.

Furthermore, notwithstanding R. C. Sproul's earlier praise of Arminius' adherence to some Calvinist beliefs, Sproul suggests blatant areas of divergence between Arminius and Calvin. Speaking of Arminius' understanding that regeneration is progressive, he writes, "If he [Arminius] means that the work of regeneration is not instantaneous but gradual, then he sets himself in opposition to Reformation thought."[26] Sproul also suggests, "For the Reformers, the internal call is effectual. That is, all who God calls internally comply with his call . . . Arminius makes it clear that prevenient grace is resistible."[27]

This understanding of Arminius clearly goes against Calvinist thought. Peterson and Williams also conclude that Arminius' belief of the synergistic nature of regeneration contrary to the one-sided, monergistic belief of Calvinism as another key difference. They state, "Arminians also argue for universal prevenient

---

24. Rice, "Divine Knowledge and Free-Will Theism," 133.
25. Calvin, *Institutes*, 926.
26. Sproul, *Willing to Believe*, 129.
27. Ibid., 130.

grace from synergism, their view that God and sinners (enabled by grace) cooperate in salvation."[28]

Cameron presents additional important differences between Arminius and Calvinism. He suggests that the main difference between the two is "... not between determinism and free will. Rather, it is the contrast between grace and sin."[29] Contrary to Calvinist thought, Arminius thought that God called all humanity to believe and that he provided sufficient grace for all to respond. Although this position seemingly acquits Arminius from the heresy of Pelagianism, it is still in disagreement with Reformed thought because resistance to the grace of God could make divine efforts ineffective. This implies that God is not always omnipotent—a position contrary to Reformed thought.

Lutzer supplements this understanding of Arminius' departure from Calvinist thought when he says, "He [Arminius] and his followers took a more moderate position regarding original sin and drafted five articles that were more in tune with Semi-Pelagianism than Calvinism."[30] For the Calvinist, "God must regenerate him [all humanity] and even grant him the faith to believe. In contrast, Arminianism teaches that man is to some degree depraved, but that he receives enough grace to counteract the effects of depravity."[31] In Lutzer's mind, Arminius' position on the role of humanity undoubtedly departs from mainstream Reformed thought.

Finally, Carl Bangs also indicates clear differences between Arminius and Calvinism. Calvinism states that God's grace is irresistible. According to Bangs, Arminius felt, "Grace is not a force; it is a Person, the Holy Spirit, and in personal relationships there cannot be the sheer overpowering of one person by another."[32]

Mainstream Calvinism would not agree to this supposition. If God is all-powerful, then no one can successfully resist Him unless God permits it to occur. Peterson and Williams assert, "How

---

28. Peterson and Anderson, *Why I Am Not an Arminian*, 183.
29. Cameron, "Arminius—Hero or Heretic?" 219.
30. Lutzer, *The Doctrines That Divide*, 178.
31. Ibid., 180.
32. Bangs, *Arminius*, 343.

can Calvinists say that God's grace is irresistible? The answer is that we don't teach that God's grace is irresistible for all; rather, God's grace is irresistible only for God's people. God's invincible grace eventually brings all of the elect to salvation."[33]

This concept leads Bangs to another point of disparity between Arminius and Calvinism. It is Bangs assertion that Arminius further fell out of line with mainstream Calvinism concerning the doctrinal understandings of assurance of salvation and the perseverance of the saints—two doctrines for the Supralapsarians that logically followed a deterministic understanding of predestination. Bangs writes, "Arminius felt that Supralapsarianism led to either unwarranted security or unwarranted despair."[34] The determinism of the Calvinists seemed too restrictive of God's love for Arminius' liking and so he chose a looser interpretation of election, deciding to focus on "some" instead of "each man."[35]

A Declaration's Call For Reconciliation and Unity

Arminius was careful to conclude *A Declaration of Sentiments* with an entreaty for reconciliation and unity with his Christian countrymen, regardless if they were also his adversaries. Many scholars have noted this compassionate appeal of Arminius and find it note-worthy.

Wood states that at the end of *A Declaration*, "Arminius pleads for charity and a degree of fraternal unity within the Dutch Church as theological discussion continues."[36] Furthermore, if Arminius' views were found unacceptable, Arminius claimed he would, for the sake of unity, resign as professor at Leyden. According to Wood, Arminius presented his Declaration ". . . with the intention of reaching a resolution."[37]

---

33. Peterson and Williams, *Why I Am Not an Arminian*, 185.
34. Ibid., 347.
35. Calvin, *Institutes*, 926.
36. Wood, "The Declaration of Sentiments," 128.
37. Ibid., 114.

Bangs also alludes to the fraternal spirit of Arminius at the end of his treatise. Bangs first describes the commitment that Arminius makes to abide by the decision of the Assembly and then expresses Arminius' confidence that "He [Arminius] is sure that if his brethren will adopt the same point of view, there will be no controversy."[38] From Bangs' examination and analysis of *A Declaration*, it is clear that he believes that one of Arminius' main goals was to recover unity with all members of the Reformed Church. This goal is why Arminius elects to speak in front of the Assembly and is why he presents his arguments so passionately. He wishes to end the dissension with his fellow-Believers.

Cameron also notes Arminius' call for healing in *A Declaration of Sentiments*. Cameron states, "We should pay close attention to Arminius' concern with reconciliation."[39] He further points to Arminius' awareness of the dangers of erring in the religious sphere. If one errs theologically, not only is it difficult to discern what the problem ultimately concerns, it can hamper kindness toward one another and can cause factionalism within a group and hypocritical behavior. Cameron adds, "Arminius seeks to strengthen the true believer's assurance of salvation without giving any encouragement to a false assurance."[40]

Lastly, Jacobsen proposes several conclusions that can be drawn from Arminius' insight into dealing with controversy as demonstrated in *A Declaration*. Jacobsen summarizes Arminius' advice for healthy reconciliation in three parts. First, all parties involved in this controversy need to set aside all "biased judgmentalism" regarding their opponents. Second, the reality and limitations of every investigation must be acknowledged. God is omniscient, but no theologian can share that label with Him. Thus, growth can occur on both sides of the issue. Third, despite interpretational differences, an "ecumenical dialogue" needs to be maintained.[41]

---

38. Bangs, *Arminius*, 316.
39. Cameron, "Arminius—Hero or Heretic?" 214.
40. Ibid., 226.
41. Jacobsen, "The Calvinist-Arminian Dialectic," 78.

Jacobsen's understanding mirrors Arminius' philosophy well as observed in *A Declaration*. He continues, "Arminius thought that Christian fellowship ought to be maintained between parties that differed from each other—even over matters of salvation."[42] Interestingly, Jacobsen's summary of Arminius' sentiments seem to have a postmodern feel about it despite Arminius' words being conceived over four hundred years ago.

The scholastic debate over Arminius and his *Declaration of Sentiments* has been in existence since *A Declaration*'s delivery in 1608. Arminius advocated for doctrines that paradoxically appear to be both part of and yet different from the Calvinist Reformed tradition. However, whether in complete disagreement with Calvinism or by merely being just a unique expression of that theological belief system, Arminius trusted (some say foolishly)[43] that his suggestions would bring healing and focus to a religious scene full of controversy and frustration.

Despite coming from differing theological camps, the preceding scholars' appraisals demonstrate the overall quality and achievement of Arminius' theological presentation in *A Declaration of Sentiments*. Like Arminius and the Supralapsarians, Scripture and interpretational standards limit these scholars' understandings, but they still offer valuable insight into how well Arminius defended himself and his theology against the Supralapsarians. No doubt future students of Arminius may contribute more to this investigation in areas that appear unexamined. The next chapter will focus on a few of these unexamined areas.

---

42. Ibid., 81.
43. Bangs, *Arminius*, 316.

7

Reflections Upon the Man and His Manuscript

THE PREVIOUS CHAPTER EXAMINED the opinions of several scholars and theologians concerning assorted factors involved in Arminius' attempt to defend himself in his *Declaration of Sentiments* against the Supralapsarian party. Although these researchers have offered much to consider regarding Arminius and his treatise, their investigations may be augmented with additional elements of consideration for a fuller analysis of *A Declaration*. This particular chapter is by no means the conclusion of this book; rather, it is more of a supplement for significant aspects concerning Arminius that may deserve mentioning. As such, four apparently unexplored aspects significant for understanding the relationship of Arminius, *A Declaration*, and the Supralapsarians will be presented. Once again, to maintain a proper sense of balance, two of the aspects will show critiques of Arminius and *A Declaration* and the other two will show approbations.

Reflections Upon the Man and His Manuscript

Two Critiques of Arminius and A Declaration

Innocent or Instigator?

Since *A Declaration* was written as a defense, it is impossible not to note specific self-protective statements of Arminius occurring regularly. These comments present him claiming complete innocence in his conflict with the Supralapsarians. He made statements such as, "I should never afford either cause or occasion for schism and separation, in the Church of God or in our common country;"[1] "I gave in common my usual answer, 'that they had no reason for demanding such an account from me, rather than from others;'"[2] and "that there is no cause whatever for preferring an accusation against me on account of my behavior throughout these transactions."[3]

Although the absolute degree of responsibility on either side of this controversy is indeterminable, the one-sidedness of the controversy, according to Arminius' suggestions in *A Declaration*, seems implausible. No doubt this was part of the scholarly tactics of the day, but by relying on this approach, Arminius' character, objectivity, and argument was diminished. He claimed to be above reproach, and yet, his very own words within *A Declaration* suggest a different conclusion—threatening his credibility.

As explained in earlier chapters, there were people who sought to destroy Arminius (at least vocationally) and eradicate his theological influence; however, Arminius, too, strived to denounce his attackers and the error of their theological understandings. In his introductory address in *A Declaration*, he states, "Such an erroneous statement might also have been made, either through the inconsiderateness which arises from a defect in the intellect, through a weakness of an imperfect memory, or through a prejudice of the affections."[4]

---

1. Arminius, *A Declaration of Sentiments*, 5.
2. Ibid., 26.
3. Ibid., 37.
4. Ibid., 44.

Basically, he called his Supralapsarian opponents stupid, senile, biased, and unable to behave morally in this controversy. Remarks like these appear to be a personal provocation on Arminius' part, suggesting that he was indeed part of the controversy.

Supporting his attitude of complete innocence, Arminius uses terms such as "sinister,"[5] "carefully concealed,"[6] "groundless suspicions,"[7] "oppressing me,"[8] and the like to suggest first, that a conspiracy was at work against him, and second, that he was a blameless victim.

In this psychological and theological drama, Arminius presented this controversy as though the Supralapsarians caused all the conflict and that he merely dodged their blows. The evidence suggests something different. Rarely in life is a conflict so one-sided.

An Imbalanced Examination

Another critical factor of Arminius and his *A Declaration* concerns the lopsided examination of several topics within his defense treatise. He was called before the Assembly to ". . . make an open and bona fide declaration of all [his] sentiments, views, and designs on every subject connected with Religion."[9] While Arminius did superficially accomplish this goal, his efforts appear somewhat calculated and/or diversionary.

With his exhaustive presentation of the errors of the Supralapsarian understanding of predestination, it would seem probable that he would also provide in-depth examinations of other topics of controversy. However, most of the sections in *A Declaration* are merely one-to-two pages in length, and the contents frequently are a bare-boned deliberation on a topic.

---

5. Ibid., 6.
6. Ibid., 21.
7. Ibid., 48.
8. Ibid., 53.
9. Ibid., 5.

Additionally, Arminius' examination of these topics often strays from his earlier expressed purpose to incidental matters of a political rather than a theological nature. An example of this is Section IX of *A Declaration* where he began discussing justification, but very shortly thereafter began discussing a dispute between two other parties.

While it is true that Arminius had only ten days to write his defense, he also had several years to consider each theological topic. By focusing predominantly on the Supralapsarian controversy, Arminius neglected other equally deserving (and neglected) doctrines upon which he might have expounded. Doctrines such as the assurance of salvation and perseverance of the saints (Section V–VI), if explained more fully, could have provided extra support in his defense against the high Calvinists.

Two Approbations of Arminius and A Declaration

Despite the previous criticisms of Arminius and *A Declaration*, clear, positive factors concerning Arminius and his treatise may also have been overlooked. These aspects add support to the validity of Arminius' defense against the High Calvinists and help in our analysis and understanding of *A Declaration*.

The Mystery of God

The first positive point concerns Arminius' appeal to the mystery of God. In *A Declaration*, he judged the Supralapsarians harshly because their extra-biblical assumptions of doctrine surpassed Scripture in many ways. Much of the mystery of God and His ways were being explained away—something a finite being cannot do without the express help of God. Commenting on the predestination of each individual, Arminius remarks,

> Nay, this doctrine does not even teach what kind of men in general God has predestinated, which is properly the doctrine of the Gospel; but it embraces within itself a

certain mystery, which is known only to God, who is the Predestinater, and in which mystery are comprehended what particular persons and how many he has decreed to save and to condemn.[10]

Arminius was suggesting that the Supralapsarians had erred in their over-reliance upon reason and logic. By this time, the biblical canon was closed, but their attitude implied that Calvin's *Institutes* were as great as the Gospels and Epistles. Arminius felt this outlook was wrong because God had divinely created the Bible, and the *Institutes* were a man-made creation.

Nevertheless, the Reformers' utilization of scholasticism was beneficial in comprehending theological matters to some degree. Peterson and Williams state, "The revival of scholasticism introduced into Reformed theology a greater emphasis upon philosophical and metaphysical concerns than Calvin entertained."[11] Still, where paradox and mystery are present, logic fails.

One cannot use logic alone to explain how Jesus can be simultaneously both human and divine nor use it to explicate the "individual-yet-one" existence of the Trinity, nor fully understand how a person can be part of God's irresistible plan and yet still have a free will. The reality is that God's ways are mysterious and unexplainable at times. In *A Declaration*, Arminius frequently appealed to this concept in his defense against the high Calvinists.

The Loving Grace of God

Finally, and most importantly, Arminius' *A Declaration* does an admirable job of elaborating on the love of God, especially concerning His gift of divine grace to those in need. A quick survey of *A Declaration* will demonstrate that Arminius used the term, "Divine Grace," in eight out of the ten sections in this treatise.[12] Apparently, he wanted the Assembly to know how pivotal the

---

10. Ibid., 76.
11. Peterson and Williams, *Why I Am Not an Arminian*, 93.
12. *A Declaration*, Sections 1, 3–7, and 9.

grace of God is in human existence—and in his defense against the Supralapsarians.

According to Arminius, without grace, nothing good could happen—absolutely nothing. God's grace is the sole/soul source for eternal justification—it is unearned, unmerited, and unconditional for everyone. Yet, the Bible also speaks of free will of those choosing to improve upon their spiritual walks by embracing the ongoing sanctification of God.

Here, of course, is where Arminius departed from his Supralapsarian brethren, but he departed to defend the love of God for the whole world—saint, sinner, and Spaniard[13] alike. This is a position he saw substantiated in Scripture and in society. It is also a position to be highlighted, for with it, he presented the biblical character of God more persuasively than do the Supralapsarians.

No doubt the high Calvinists considered his position soft and too inclusive; however, Arminius never suggests universalism. Just like the adage that suggest that without justice, love is ineffective and sentimental, while justice without love is rigid and heartless, so Arminius' *Declaration* affirms that the sinner is separated from the love of God except through the grace of God in Jesus Christ. It also upholds that the love and grace of God are available for the chosen that will not resist it.

Such an optimistic approach is characteristic of Arminius and his *Declaration*. However, the criticisms discussed earlier of him and his work cannot be ignored. In striving to better understand the man and his treatise, all factors of his character and writing need to be examined. Focusing on either just the positive or the negative aspects alone can lead to naive hero-worship or obtuse condemnation. More likely, the truth lies somewhere between these two extremes.

---

13. See chapter two for more details of the Spanish involvement in Holland.

8

Final Thoughts

Summary

THE PRECEDING CHAPTERS HAVE provided numerous aspects for examination concerning Arminius and *A Declaration of Sentiments*. Like pieces in a jigsaw puzzle that are carefully placed for an ever-fuller picture of the object of study, each chapter was designed to provide a better understanding of Arminius' motivation and goals for the creation of *A Declaration*.

To provide a better comprehension of the conflict between Arminius and the high Calvinists, this examination began with a general overview of the surrounding cultures active at the time of Arminius. This Dutch reformer did not merely sit down and write *A Declaration* void of outside encouragement; several different aspects of culture, politics, and society surrounded him.

Although he certainly had a unique and talented personality, Arminius' hopes, goals, and priorities were shaped by numerous specific forces in his life—such as the Dutch-Spanish conflict for independence, the re-emergence of scholasticism, and the Calvinist theocratic ideal of civil structure. Factors such as these were a

Final Thoughts

perpetual catalyst for Arminius' controversial dialogue and dealings with Supralapsarians throughout his life.

This book's goal was further defined by investigating the characters involved in Arminius' life from childhood through adulthood. Early on, specific characters (both friend and foe) helped to cultivate and encourage Arminius in his endeavors to become an excellent scholar and theologian. They provided the support and resistance that initially helped to sharpen his responses to theological matters. By the turn of the seventeenth-century, however, other of these key figures touched his life more dramatically, forcing him through political and theological means into an on-going debate over Reformed theology.

The final result of this dispute was a presentation to the States General assembly at The Hague. After examining the culture and people involved in Arminius' life, this treatise began a general inspection of *A Declaration of Sentiments*. This took the form of a broad survey of various factors including the purpose of the document as a defense against high Calvinist condemnation, a description of its theological and civil audience, a brief synopsis of *A Declaration's* contents and the controversial topics it addressed, and the ultimate results of Arminius' presentation. The goal simply was to provide an overview of *A Declaration* before specifically focusing on the weighty details and sophisticated theological arguments that lay within its pages.

Following this, an intensive analysis and breakdown of *A Declaration's* contents, section by section, was begun. The goal of this chapter was to provide an ample understanding of Arminius' theological defense against the Supralapsarians. Each section of *A Declaration* was inspected in its refutation of high Calvinist condemnation or as a proof for keeping with Reformed thought.

The next chapter focused on scholarly opinions available regarding Arminius and his *Declaration*. Critiques of several prominent theologians and historians were offered for consideration regarding Arminius' responses in *A Declaration* to matters of doctrine, his maintenance and departure from Reformed Calvinist thought, and his appeal for unity and reconciliation. In each of these areas, an attempt was made to maintain balance by providing examples on both sides of the issues. The overall goal was to offer the reader unbiased information for possible use in later judgment on Arminius and his work. Despite some critical weaknesses, overall, various scholars judged *A Declaration* a clearly-written and somewhat successful defense against Supralapsarian charges.

Finally, the study turned to some areas of interest not fully addressed by the scholars. Two critical opinions were given, followed by two affirmations of his work. These judgments were additionally provided to help the goal of a more complete picture of Arminius and *A Declaration*.

Conclusion

Much has been said regarding Arminius and *A Declaration of Sentiments*, and clearly much more could and will be added in the decades to come. Scholars like Carl Bangs, W. Stephen Gunter, Roger Olson, R.C. Sproul, Vic Reasoner, etc. have invested significant portions of their professional lives studying this famous Dutch theologian and his sometimes-controversial ideas. Hopefully, this book has offered a sufficient examination and analysis of Arminius and his treatise so that readers can say with confidence that they have a better understanding of Arminius' *Declaration of Sentiments* and its defense against Supralapsarian attacks.

A Declaration of Sentiments is not merely a theological treatise on Reformed thought; rather, it is the final testament of Jacobus Arminius in his pursuit for doctrinal purity and peaceful relations with the high Calvinists. Due to the complexity of his times and the Supralapsarian controversy surrounding Arminius, it is difficult to determine how successful he was in this endeavor. However, if nothing else, on October 30, 1608, Arminius effectively held the attention of the Assembly and proclaimed his understanding of Scriptural and doctrinal truths in *A Declaration of Sentiments*.

The introduction of this study alluded to the controversial conflict between Arminianism and Calvinism. Both sides claimed to be true representatives of God's Word, and both claimed that

Final Thoughts

the other side was mistaken in their doctrinal understandings. As Bang writes, "The result would be a growing polarity, or perhaps more accurately a growing recognition of polarity, between [these] two broad parties within the Dutch Reformed Church."[1] Complicating matters more, each group proclaimed their respective five-point synopsis of beliefs *ex cathedra* while claiming approval from their namesakes, which is debatable.

As we have learned, though, this approval may not be completely valid in either case. Many Calvinists often end up hating Jacobus Arminius for his heresies, and some Arminians similarly despise Jean Calvin, considering him to be an unloving religious despot. Unfortunately, their rejections may not be wholly based on historical or theological truth, and assumptions mistakenly become convictions with improper evidence and unfair judgments.

It is, of course, acceptable to reject or approve of Jacobus Arminius and his *Declaration of Sentiments* dependent upon one's theological or scriptural position. Hopefully, though, this book has provided a balanced analysis to enable that choice to be based more on historical and biblical fact rather than on rumor or speculation. Truly, this is all Arminius would have asked of his critics.

---

1. Bangs, "Arminius as a Reformed Theologian," 214.

Afterword

HISTORICALLY, IT HAS BEEN easier to dismiss Arminius than to give him a fair hearing. John S. Knox has introduced the significance of Arminius and his theology in this short book. Between 2010 and 2013, six installments by Knox were published in *The Arminian Magazine*, which I edit. They were published under the title, "Getting Acquainted with Arminius."[1] Essentially, Knox summarized *Declaration of Sentiments*. Then, in the Spring 2016 issue, Knox had a companion article on Gomarus.[2] I am happy to see these articles woven together and expanded into *Jacobus Arminius Stands His Ground: A Declaration Against High Calvinism*.

From the Remonstrants to the present day, those who admire Arminius fall into four categories:

- Reformed Arminian. See Roger E. Olson, *Arminian Theology: Myths and Realities* (InterVarsity, 2006); J. Matthew Pinson, *Arminian and Baptist* (Randall House, 2015); Robert E. Picirilli, *Free Will Revisited: A Respectful Response to Luther, Calvin, and Edwards* (Wipf & Stock, 2017).

- Stone-Campbell Restoration Arminian. In this tradition, Jack Cottrell is always worth reading.

- Anabaptist Arminians. Waldensians and other groups prior to the Reformation affirmed that each person may choose the contingent response of either resisting God's grace or

---

1. Knox, "Getting Acquainted With Arminius, Part 1," 9.
2. Knox, "Franciscus Gomarus," 24.

yielding to it. This belief was also affirmed by Anabaptist-Mennonite movement.

- Wesleyan-Arminian is my preferred label. Ironically, Wesley lived in the eighteenth century, while the life of Arminius spanned the sixteenth and seventeenth centuries — yet, Wesley's name comes first!

It was Wesley who launched *The Arminian Magazine* in 1778. As the first editor, Wesley's purpose was for the magazine to serve "principally as an engine of polemical theology."[3] While the name of the magazine changed to *The Methodist Magazine* in 1798, the Wesleyan-Arminian message was so successfully propagated that by the turn of the twentieth century, it was assumed by many that Calvinism had expired. In 1902, Milton S. Terry complained that undue attention was devoted "to the issues of old Calvinist and Arminian controversies, which ought to be now considered obsolete."[4]

However, I must express my profound concern that there are significant differences between early Methodist theology and the later American holiness movement. This problem is confounded by the fact that the American holiness movement claims to be "Wesleyan," but is much closer to Charles Finney. I would prefer to exclude Finney from this list of Arminian options on the basis that he is more properly a Pelagian. I would also reject open theism as an orthodox Arminian option, but my analysis is not universally accepted.

Although Milton S. Terry reported things the way he saw them at the turn of the twentieth century, he did not foresee the rise of the "young, restless, and reformed" resurgence, reported by *Christianity Today* in 2006.[5] Among those of us who are "old and rested" Arminians, I am delighted to see the push back.

---

3. Whedon, *Methodist Quarterly Review*, 381.
4. Terry, *Doctrines of Christian Experience*, 7.
5. Hansen, "Young, Restless, Reformed," 32.

Jacobus Arminius Stands His Ground

In 2012, Keith D. Stanglin and Thomas H. McCall wrote the new standard: *Jacob Arminius: Theologian of Grace* (Oxford University Press, 2012), but I am watching such authors as Gil VanOrder, Jr.[6] and John S. Knox very carefully taking aim at the new Calvinistic consensus.

Solomon observed, "There is no end to the making of many books, and much study is exhausting to the body" (Eccl 12:12). Yet, more books are preferable to academic censorship and the closed shop which Arminius faced. As Knox has shown in this book, Calvinism had become rigid and rationalistic. And when everyone is on the same page, perhaps something is being omitted.

The godly John Fletcher published essays on both "Biblical Calvinism" and "Biblical Arminianism" in 1777. He warned that rigid Calvinism led to lawlessness and rigid Arminianism led to legalism. He explained, "The most effectual, not to say the *only* way of ending these theological disputes of Christians, and destroying the errors of leveling Pelagianism, antinomian Calvinism, confused Arminianism, and reprobating Popery, is to restore primitive harmony and fullness to the partial gospels of the day."[7]

In other words, Fletcher said that every position had a corner on truth—but they all held tenaciously to different corners! That resulted in a "partial gospel" in the eighteenth century. Fletcher concluded by suggesting that Pharisaism needed the antidote of Bible Calvinism and their doctrines of grace. Antinomianism needed the antidote of Bible Arminianism and their doctrine of justice.

Things are no different today. For too long, Arminius has been the "scapegoat of Calvinism" (to borrow from the title of a lecture I gave in 1998). In 2012, Stephen Gunter wrote, "Ironically, Arminius is important again because the misrepresentation of his teachings is the favorite whipping boy of the aggressive New Calvinism."[8] But Arminius was merely trying to correct some of the excesses that had developed because they had a theological monopoly.

---

6. VanOrder, *Can You Trust in Jesus?* (2017).
7. Fletcher, *The Works of the Rev. John Fletcher*, 364.
8. Gunter, *Arminius and His Declaration of Sentiments*, 4.

Afterword

Yet, the theological heirs of Arminius have sometimes needed their feet held to the fire. Everything we believe in must be examined on the basis of the final authority of Scripture. Anyone who can calmly and patiently show me where I have missed the way is my friend. Perhaps this brief book by John S. Knox will help both Arminians and Calvinists get to the heart of the debate.

Vic Reasoner
President, Southern Methodist College
Editor, *The Arminian Magazine* (since 1993)

Glossary

Arminianism: Followers generally follow the theological ideas of the Remonstrants (and loosely Arminius' doctrinal understandings): Human beings, despite their fallen nature, can freely choose God on their own; God chose people for salvation or perdition based on foreknowledge of their response to the Good News; Jesus Christ died for the sins of all humanity—not just the Elect; human beings can resist the grace of God and reject his salvation gift; and finally, human beings can lose their salvation even if they once believed.

Belgic Confession: Also known as the Dutch Confession, it was composed by Walloon pastor-theologian Guido de Bres (1522–1567), a student of Calvin and Beza in Geneva. The Confession includes thirty-seven articles that deal with doctrinal matters concerning God, Scripture, humanity, sin, Christ, salvation, the church, and eschatology.

Catechism: An official doctrinal statement of a Christian group used to instruct and direct followers within that movement.

Council of Troubles: Also known as the Council of Blood (1567–1574), it was a court established in the Low Countries by the Spanish governor, the Duke of Alba, during the Revolt of the Netherlands to suppress Protestantism and particularism.

A Declaration of Sentiments on Predestination: Dutch Reformer Jacobus Arminius' written defense to the Assembly at the Hague regarding his theological views, which were under attack by the

Glossary

Supralapsarians (the High Calvinists). With A Declaration, Arminius attempted to highlight the political wrong-doings of the European Protestant church and its extremist theological understandings of certain Christian doctrines such as predestination.

The Fall: When Adam and Eve ate of the fruit of the Tree of Knowledge of Good and Evil in disobedience, thus destroying their perfect harmonious relationship with God and leading to their expulsion from the Garden of Eden, painful child-bearing for women, laborious agricultural toiling for men, and the eventual death of Adam, Eve, and all humanity (so Genesis 3).

Free Will: The human capacity to act as one wishes without being controlled by God (so Proverbs 16:9).

The Hague: The seat of government and administrative center of the Netherlands, on the North Sea coast, the capital of the province of South Holland.

Heidelberg Catechism: Written in 1563, it is often called the Palantinate Catechism and includes 129 questions and answers over the Fall, human depravity, redemption, the importance of faith, justification by faith, the Sacraments, the keys of the kingdom, conversion, the Decalogue, and the Lord's Prayer.

High Calvinism: Also known as hyper-Calvinism, the Supralapsarians fell into this theological camp and believed that all soteriological questions (personal salvation) had already been decided by God before the creation of the world.

Infralapsarians: Infralapsarians ("after the Fall") held that God first decided whom he would allow into the world and second that he would then save people from it.

The Institutes: Originally one book, it evolved into four books on proper Protestant doctrine concerning God the Creator, redemption mediated through Christ, appropriation of redemption, and the church's relationship to greater society. In an attempt to provide

GLOSSARY

assurance or confidence in one's salvation, Calvin elaborated on why people believe in the Christian, biblical message or not—thus, focusing on the doctrine of Predestination.

Monergism: The belief that the work of salvation is by God alone (so Ephesians 2:8).

The Netherlands: Also known as Holland, it is a northwestern European country known for its shipping, canals, tulips, and windmills.

Pelagianism: Named after a monk in the fifth century, CE, Pelagianism asserts that Adam's original sin was not passed on to all generations of humanity. Thus, somewhat like in Islam, people are born innocent, free from sin, and then proceed (potentially but not absolutely) to volitionally choose to do evil.

Perseverance of the Saints: Popularly defined as "once saved, always saved," this doctrine suggests that once people are born again with the indwelling of the Holy Spirit, they will never stop believing even if they stumble, and God will never desert them (so Hebrews 13:5).

The Plague: A pandemic that swept across Europe in the fourteenth century, it is caused by a bacterium that produces huge swelling in the lymph nodes, fever, pneumonic symptoms, severe headaches, diarrhea, and eventual death. It is thought that nearly twenty million people died from the disease in Europe, including one half of all the Christian clergy, leading to terrific changes in European society.

Predestination: The concept that all human and natural events have already been decided in advance by God (so Ephesians 1:4–5).

Protestantism: The branch of Christianity that rose in the sixteenth century as a backlash against the abuses and excesses of the Roman Catholic Church and her leaders. Rather than focusing on episcopal authority, Protestantism considers scripture to be the ultimate authority in life, only behind Jesus Christ, the Son of God.

Glossary

Providence: God's implementation of his will in determining or controlling human affairs as well as earthly and celestial events (so Psalm 103:19).

The Reformation: Although many people contributed to this movement (Wycliffe, Huss, Erasmus, Calvin, Zwingli), German Professor-Priest-Monk Martin Luther is attributed with being its main founder when he nailed his *Ninety-five Theses* to the Wittenberg church door in 1517. Luther (and other reformers) promoted the primacy of scripture (sola scriptura) and faith in Jesus (sola fide) as the only avenue for forgiveness and salvation. Good works and obedience to church leaders were not part of the justification formula although they could be part of sanctification of believers.

The Remonstrants: Under the guidance of Hans Uytenbogaert and Simon Episcopus, nearly fifty proponents of Arminius' theology met in Gouda in 1610 to officially compose a statement of faith based on the Dutch Reformer's theological understandings. They concluded the following: 1. God has decreed to save through Jesus Christ those of the fallen and sinful race who through the grace of the Holy Spirit believe in him, but leaves in sin the incorrigible and unbelieving. 2. Christ died for all humanity (not just for the elect), but no one except the believer has remission of sin. 3. Man or Woman can neither of themselves nor of their free will do anything truly good until they are born again of God, in Christ, through the Holy Spirit. 4. All good deeds or movements in the regenerate must be ascribed to the grace of God but his grace is not irresistible. 5.Those who are incorporated into Christ by a true faith have power given them through the assisting grace of the Holy Spirit to persevere in the faith. But it is possible for a believer to fall from grace.

Reprobation: The concept that, regarding predestination and the will of God, an unknown number of human beings (called the reprobate) have been created and predestined to be condemned to eternal damnation for their errors and disobedience (so 2 Thessalonians 2:12).

Glossary

Sabellianism: An alternative name for the Modalist form of Monarchianism—God first existed as the Father, then the Son, and now as the Holy Spirit.

Scholasticism: The method of study in the Middle Ages used to support the doctrines of the church through reason and logic.

Socinian: A Reformation-era heresy that denied Christ's deity, substitutionary atonement, and God's foreknowledge and foreordination.

Supralapsarians: Hold the position that God first decided that he would save some people and then second that he would allow sin into the world. By contrast, the infralapsarian ("after the Fall") position is the reverse in that it holds that God first decided he would allow sin into the world and second that he would then save people from it.

Synergism: The belief that the accomplishment of salvation involves cooperation between God and humanity (so Joshua 24:14–15).

Synod of Dort: Held in Dordrecht in 1618–1619, this international gathering, supervised and sponsored by the Dutch Reformed Church, met to discuss and deal with the controversy of Arminianism and the Remonstrants' Articles of Faith.

Tritheism: The heretical teaching about the Trinity that denies the unity of substance in the Divine Persons.

TULIP: The traditional five points of Calvinism (associated with the acronym "TULIP") was commissioned by the Dutch Reformed Church and composed during the Synod of Dordt (1618–1619), which met in Dordrecht, South Holland. The religious assembly penned eighteen articles on proper Reformed doctrine that can be condensed to five main ideas, which challenged the five theological assertions of the Remonstrants. TULIP stands for total depravity, unconditional election, limited atonement, irresistible grace, and the perseverance of the saints.

Glossary

Universalism: The doctrinal understanding that all people in history, regardless of their beliefs and actions, will be saved from eternal damnation or divine judgment after death, whether due to the atonement of Jesus Christ or the inherent goodness of human beings made in God's image.

Additional Notes on A Declaration

Section 1: "On Predestination"

_____
_____
_____
_____
_____
_____
_____
_____
_____
_____

Section 2: "The Providence of God"

_____
_____
_____
_____
_____
_____

Additional Notes on A Declaration

Section 3: "The Free-Will of Man"

Section 4: "The Grace of God"

Additional Notes on a Declaration

Section 5: "The Perseverance of the Saints"

Section 6: "The Assurance of Salvation"

Additional Notes on A Declaration

Section 7: "The Perfection of Believers in This Life"

Section 8: "The Divinity of the Son of God"

Additional Notes on A Declaration

Section 9: "The Justification of Man Before God"

Section 10: "The Revision of the Dutch Confession and the Heidelberg Catechism"

Bibliography

Arminius, James. *A Declaration of Sentiments on Predestination.* Online: Two Sparrows, 2014.
_____. "Letter to Sebastian Egbertz, May 3, 1607." 236–237. In *Praestantium ec Eruditorum Virorum Epistolae Ecclesiasticae et Theologicae.* Amsterdam, 1660.
_____. "The Works of Jacobus Arminius." *God Rules,* June 17, 2018. Online: http://www.godrules.net/library/arminius/arminius.htm#public-disputations.
The Works of James Arminius. James Nichols and William Nichols, trans. Grand Rapids, MI: Baker, 1999.
Bangs, Carl. *Arminius: A Study in the Dutch Reformation.* New York, NY: Abingdon, 1971.
_____. "Arminius as a Reformed Theologian." In *The Heritage of John Calvin: Heritage Hall Lectures, 1960-70.* John H. Bratt, ed. Grand Rapids, MI: Eerdmans, 1973.
Barth, Karl. "The Doctrine of God." In *Church Dogmatics,* Vol. 2, Part 2. G.W. Bromiley and T.F Torrance, eds. Edinburgh, SC: T & T Clark, 1957.
Basinger, Randall. "Divine Sovereignty: What Difference Does It Make?" *The Evangelical Quarterly* 5, no. 1 (1987) 15–30.
Bertius, Petrus. *Hymenaeus Desertor, Sive de Sanctorum Apostasia Problemata Duo.* Ghent, BE: Joannis Patii, 1601.
Bloesch, Donald G. *Essentials of Evangelical Theology,* Vol 2. San Francisco, CA: HarperSanFrancisco, 2001.
Boettner, Loraine. *The Reformed Doctrine of Predestination.* Philadelphia, PA: The Presbyterian and Reformed Publishing Company, 1966.
Bratt, John. *The Heritage of John Calvin.* USA: Calvin College and Seminary, 1973.
Bray, John S. *Theodore Beza's Doctrine of Predestination.* Nieuwkoop, NL: B. De Graaf, 1975.
Brian, Rustin. *Jacob Arminius: The Man from Oudewater.* Eugene, OR: Wipf and Stock, 2015.

BIBLIOGRAPHY

Brown, Colin. "Scholasticism." In *Introduction to the History of Christianity*. Tim Dowley, ed. 286-287. Minneapolis, MN: Fortress, 2006.

Brunner, Daniel. "Lecture: Jacob Arminius and the Remonstrants." *CHT512*. Portland, OR: George Fox Seminary, 2001.

Bryant, Barry E. "Molina, Arminius, Plaifere, Goad, and Wesley in Human Freewill, Divine Omniscience, and Middle Knowledge." *Wesleyan Theological Journal* 27, no. 1-2 (1992) 93-103.

Calvin, John. *Commentary on John*, Vol. 1 (John 1-10) & Vol. 2 (John 11-21). T. F. and D.W. Torrance, eds. T.H.L. Parker, trans. Edinburgh, SC: Oliver and Boyd, 1959 & 1961.

_____. *The Mystery of Godliness*. Pennsylvania, PA: Soli Deo Gloria Ministries, 1999.

_____. *Institutes of the Christian Religion*, Vol 1 and Vol 2. John T. McNeill, ed. Ford L. Battles, trans. Philadelphia, PA: Westminster, 1975.

Cameron, Charles M. "Arminius—Hero or Heretic?" *The Evangelical Quarterly* 64, no. 3 (1992) 213-227.

Clarke, F. Stuart. "Arminius' Understanding of Calvin." *The Evangelical Quarterly* 54, no. 1 (1982) 25-35.

Dekker, Eef. "Jacobus Arminius and His Logic." *The Journal of Theological Studies* 44, no. 1 (1993) 118-142.

Ellis, Mark A. *Simon Episcopius' Doctrine of Original Sin (American University Studies)*. New York, NY: Peter Lang, 2006.

Fisher, G. P. *A History of Christian Doctrine*. Philadelphia, PA: Fortress, 1978.

Fletcher, John. *The Works of the Rev. Fletcher*, Vol. 2. Salem, OH: Schmul, 1974.

Gonzalez, Justo L. *The Story of Christianity*, Vol 2. San Francisco, CA: HarperSanFrancisco, 1985.

Gottwig, Danielle Du Bois. "The Road to Seneca Falls: Elizabeth Cady Stanton and the First Woman's Rights Convention." *Fides Et Historia* 38, no. 2 (2006) 143-145.

Gunter, W. Stephen. *Arminius and His Declaration of Sentiments: An Annotated Translation with Introduction and Theological Commentary*. Waco, TX: Baylor, 2012.

Guthrie, John. *The Life of James Arminius*. Nashville, TN: Southern Methodist, 1857.

Hanko, Herman. *Portraits of Faithful Saints*. Michigan: Reformed Free Publishing Association, November 16, 2002. Online: http://www.prca.org/books/portraits/gomarus.htm.

Hansen, Collin. "Young, Restless, Reformed." *Christianity Today* 50, no. 9 (2006) 32.

Harrison, A.W. *Arminianism*. Great Britain: Kemp Hall, 1937.

_____. *The Beginnings of Arminianism*. London, UK: University of London, 1926.

Hicks, John. "Arminius on the Assurance of Salvation: The Context, Roots, and Shape of the Leiden Debate, 1603-1609." *Restoration Quarterly* 52 (2010) 50-52.

BIBLIOGRAPHY

Jacobsen, Douglas. "The Calvinist-Arminian Dialectic in Evangelical Hermeneutics." *Christian Scholar's Review* 23, no. 1 (1992) 72–89.

Kirchner, Walther. "The Duke of Alba Reconsidered." *Pacific Historical Review* 14, no. 1 (1945) 64–70.

Kirkpatrick, Daniel. *Monergism or Synergism: Is Salvation Cooperative or the Work of God Alone?* Eugene, OR: Wipf and Stock, 2018.

Knox, John S. "Franciscus Gomarus: Arminius' Adamant Adversary." *The Arminian Magazine* 34, no. 1 (Spring 2016) 3–5.

————. "Getting Acquainted With Arminius, Part 1." *The Arminian Magazine* 28, no. 2 (2010) 9–11.

————. "Getting Acquainted With Arminius, Part 2." *The Arminian Magazine* 29, no. 1 (2011) 8–10.

————. "Getting Acquainted With Arminius, Part 3." *The Arminian Magazine* 29, no. 2 (2011) 5–6.

————. "Getting Acquainted With Arminius, Part 4." *The Arminian Magazine* 30, no. 1 (2012) 5–6.

————. "Getting Acquainted With Arminius, Part 5." *The Arminian Magazine* 30, no. 2 (2012) 4–5.

————. "Getting Acquainted With Arminius, Part 6." *The Arminian Magazine* 31, no. 1 (2013) 6–7.

————. *John Wesley's 52 Standard Sermons: An Annotated Summary.* Eugene, OR: Wipf & Stock, 2017.

Lewis, C.S. *English Literature in the Sixteenth Century, Excluding Drama.* Oxford, UK: Oxford University, 1973.

Livingstone, E. A. *Oxford Concise Dictionary of the Christian Church.* Oxford, UK: Oxford University, 2000.

Lutzer, Erwin. *The Doctrines That Divide: A Fresh Look at the Historical Doctrines that Separate Christians.* Grand Rapids, MI: Kregel, 2015.

Matei-Chesnoiu, Monica. *Re-imagining Western European Geography in English Renaissance Drama.* New York, NY: Palgrave Macmillan, 2012.

McGrath, Alister E. *Historical Theology.* Great Britain: Blackwell, 2013.

McKinley, O. Glenn. *Where Two Creeds Meet.* Kansas City, MO: Beacon Hill, 1959.

"Memoirs of the Life of the Duke of Alba, Governor of the Netherlands at the Revolution under Philip II." *The Scots Magazine (1739–1803)* 51 (1789) 577–580.

Muller, Richard A. "Arminius and the Scholastic Tradition." *Calvin Theological Journal* 24, no. 1 (1989) 263–277.

————. *God, Creation, and Providence in the Thought of Jacob Arminius.* Grand Rapids, MI: Baker, 1991.

Noll, Mark A., ed. *Confessions and Catechisms of the Reformation.* Grand Rapids, MI: Baker, 1991.

Oberman, Heiko A., ed. *Studies in the History of Christian Thought,* Vol LXVI. Leiden, NL: E. J. Brill, 1995.

BIBLIOGRAPHY

"Of Predestination—by Franciscus Gomarus (1563–1641)." *Thoughts of Francis Turretin.* Online: http://turretinfan.blogspot.com/2010/04/of-predestination-gomarus.html.

Olson, Roger E. *The Story of Christian Theology: Twenty Centuries of Reform.* Downers Grove, IL: InterVarsity, 1999.

Peterson, Robert A. and Michael D. Williams. *Why I Am Not an Arminian.* Downers Grove, IL: InterVarsity, 2004.

Pettegree, Andrew, ed. *The Reformation World.* London, UK: Routledge, 2000.

Picirilli, Robert E. "Arminius and the Deity of Christ." *The Evangelical Quarterly* 70, no. 1 (1998) 51–59.

Pinnock, Clark. *Grace for All: The Arminian Dynamics of Salvation.* Eugene, OR: Wipf and Stock, 2015.

———. *The Grace of God, the Will of Man: A Case for Arminianism.* Minneapolis, MN: Bethany House, 1995.

Placher, William C. *A History of Christian Theology.* Philadelphia, PA: The Westminster Press, 1983.

Reasoner, Vic. "Arminius, the Scapegoat of Calvinism, Part 1." *The Arminian Magazine* 19, no. 1 (2001). Online: http://www.fwponline.cc/v19n1/v19n1reasoner.html.

———. "Arminius, the Scapegoat of Calvinism, Part 2." *The Arminian Magazine* 19, no. 2 (2001). Online: http://www.fwponline.cc/v19n2/v19n2reasoner.html.

———. "Arminius, the Scapegoat of Calvinism, Part 3." *The Arminian Magazine* 20, no. 1 (2002). Online: http://www.fwponline.cc/v20n1/v20n1reasoner2.htm.

Sell, Alan P. F. *The Great Debate: Calvinism, Arminianism, and Salvation.* Grand Rapids, MI: Baker, 1982.

Shirley, J. *An Epitomy of Ecclesiastical History Containing the Life and Death of Jesus Christ: With the Lives of the Apostles and Holy Evangelists.* London, UK: G. Conyers, 1706.

Spitz, L., and Barbara Tinseley. *Johann Sturm on Education: The Reformation and Humanist Learning.* St. Louis, MO: Concordia, 1995.

Sproul, R. C. *Willing to Believe: The Controversy over Free Will.* Grand Rapids, MI: Baker, 1997.

Stanglin, Keith. *Arminius on the Assurance of Salvation: The Context, Roots, and Shape of the Leiden Debate, 1603–1609.* Netherlands: Brill Academic, 2007.

———. *Jacob Arminius: Theologian of Grace.* New York, NY: Oxford University, 2012.

Studebaker, Richard. "Theological Influences on the Church: The Theology of James Arminius." Online: https://www.bethelcollege.edu/assets/content/mcarchives/pdfs/v4n2p4-17.pdf.

Swift, Dean. "The Eighty Years War & the Council of Blood." Online: http://general-history.com/the-eighty-years-war-the-council-of-blood/.

Terry, Milton. *Doctrines of Christian Experience: According to the Scriptures.* New York, NY: Eaton & Mains, 1902.

BIBLIOGRAPHY

Tillich, Paul. *A History of Christian Thought*. New York, NY: Harper & Row, 1968.

VanOrder, Gil. *Can You Trust in Jesus: Some Christians Claim You Lack the Faith?* CreateSpace, 2017.

———. *Considering Calvinism: Faith or Fatalism?* Mobile, AL: Parson Place, 2013.

Walker, Williston. *A History of the Christian Church*. New York, NY: Charles Scribner's Sons, 1959.

Wedon, D. D., ed. "The Wesleyan Methodist Magazine." *Methodist Quarterly Review* 59 (1877) 381–383.

Wood, A. Skevington. "The Declaration of Sentiments: The Theological Testament of Arminius." *The Evangelical Quarterly* 65, no. 2 (1993) 111–129.

Index

Aemilius, Theodore, 13, 17–18
Amsterdam, 7, 14, 24, 34
Arianism, 15, 56
Arminian Magazine, 76–77
Arminianism, 9, 29, 61–62, 74, 78, 81,
Augustine, Saint, 48
Αυτοθέον, 49–50
Bangs, Carl, 56, 62, 74
Baptist Arminian, 76
Belgic (or Dutch) Confession, 2, 7–8, 21, 33, 35, 52–53, 81
Bertius, Peter (the Younger), 18–20
Beza, Theodore, 1, 7, 10, 14, 25, 30,
Calvin(ism), ix, 7, 9, 14, 23–25, 34, 51, 59–63, 70, 75, 78, 83
Council of Trent, 18
Council of Troubles, 6, 81
Double Predestination (Double Election), 23, 47
Dutch Inquisition, 33
Dutch Reformed Church, 30
Dutch-Spanish Conflict, 72
Episcopius, Simon, 21
Finney, Charles, 77
Gomarus, Franciscus, xvi, 16–17, 26–28, 29, 34, 48, 57
Gunter, Stephen, 74, 78
Hague, 1, 17, 21, 32, 56, 73, 82
Heidelberg Catechism, 2, 7–8, 35, 60, 52, 82
High Calvinism, 2, 7, 60, 74, 82

Institutes of Religion, ix, 23, 51, 61, 70, 82
Justification, 2, 33, 44, 50–52, 71, 84
Koornhert, Dirck, 14
Lewis, C.S., xiii
Lubbertus, Sigrandus, 1, 30
Methodist Magazine, 77
Monergism, 43–44, 83
Netherlands, xi, 1, 6, 9, 81–83
National Synod, 21, 52
Nominalism, xii
Orange, William of, 6, 13
Pelagianism, 47, 62, 83
Perfection, 2, 47–48
Plague, 16, 83
Plancius, Petrus, 29–30
Predestination, 18, 23, 27–28, 34–35, 38–41, 47, 56–59
Prince Maurice of Nassau, 29
Providence, 41–42, 84
Reformed Arminian, 76.
Remonstrants, xi, 22, 28, 76, 81, 84
Reprobation, xii, 34, 84
Sabellianism, 49, 85
Snellius, Rudolph, 14
Socianism, 15, 20
Sproul, R.C., 2, 60–61, 74
Stone-Campbell Restoration Arminian, 76
Supralapsarian(ism), xvii, 2, 7–10, 23–26, 34–35, 38, 45, 51, 57–58, 63, 68, 70, 85

99

Index

Synod of Dort (Dordrecht), 8, 45, 60, 85
Tritheism, 49, 85
TULIP, 22, 60, 85
University of Leyden (Leiden), 1, 16, 19–20, 26

Uitenbogaert, Johannes, 20–22
Waldensian, 76
Wesleyan-Arminian, 77
Zanchius, Jerome, 25–26

www.ingramcontent.com/pod-product-compliance
Lightning Source LLC
Chambersburg PA
CBHW070928160426
43193CB00011B/1609